GW01066257

Reflections fro...
A Tongue in Ch...

Reluctantly edited by **Mark Niel**

Financial assistance is acknowledged from Arts Gateway MK – 'Funding and Support For The Arts'.

Published by: Tongue in Chic Press 2010 • ISBN: 978-0-9560974-1-5

© 2010 www.tongueinchicpoets.com • design by: david@davidbakerdesign.co.uk ~ m: +44 (0)7912 842682

Foreword

I find there's something very unnerving about being fêted as anybody that's had an influence on other people – and in 2009 I discovered that there's something even more unnerving about being hailed as (and I quote!) "The Monkeyfather of MK Poetry"! Not least being dubbed that by a great bunch of people who are nonetheless, on average, older than me! I wasn't planning on becoming an elder statesman of anything quite so early in my young life (ahem).

Still, it's always nice to be complimented I guess – though I think the super people at MK writers' group Speakeasy might quibble with any status as a visionary I may lay claim to, given that they formed in 1983 when I were a mere lad of eight wearing mismatched luminous towelling socks.

Making a lasting impression on any kind of local arts community (as *Speakeasy, Monkey Kettle, Poetry Kapow!* and now *Tongue In Chic* have) is pretty much a matter of having enough love and affection for the art form/s in question, that the hard work and financial commitment required of you don't seem an issue. 'Cos to keep plugging away at these ground-level arts schemes can burn up an awful lot of enthusiasm as the months and years roll on.

But if you're doing it right, the enthusiasm you put in should be matched by the enthusiasm others take out. What I already love about *Tongue In Chic* is that in just one year – has it really only been that since the first unforgettable night in January 2009? – they have already become established as the most inclusive, cheerful and popular poetry event I've come across in Milton Keynes. This is due in no small part to the Herculean efforts of Mr Mark Niel, himself one of the most selflessly enthusiastic people in the MK arts world.

Foreword

The genius of *Tongue In Chic* nights for me is the mixing of nervous first-time open mic-ers, relatively confident "established" local performers and seasoned performance poets from outside the borders of MK. You can almost visibly see the local writers improving with each successive event as their experience and exposure to the cream of the national poetry circuit grows. There have been some breathtaking performances already at *TiC* in its first year, and you should be able to find work by some of these poets in this very book here.

Mark and other members of the 'MK literati' (including the fandabulous *Poetry Kapow! team*) have worked so hard this year to boost their own poetry experience levels too; travelling to poetry nights in surrounding towns and cities on what seems like a more-than-weekly basis, to spread the good word and show off their wares. And bringing that experience back to Milton Keynes with them has helped so many of the local poets I've seen perform here over the last few years get better and better.

So for the first time in my Monkey Kettling years (ten and counting!) it really feels like there's an Actual Poetry Scene here in the Mirror City. Well played, *Tongue In Chic*! Here's to yer dreams! *(raises double vodka and coke in salutation)*.

matthew michael taylor esq.

A Brief History of Rhyme

I can't resist a pun and I didn't want to disappoint those of you who know me! Though this is actually a brief history of *Tongue in Chic (TiC)*, poetry in Milton Keynes by no means starts here. *TiC* is merely the latest stage of progress; building on the foundations and hard work by endeavours such as *Speakeasy, Monkey Kettle, Poetry Kapow!* and other writing groups. *Tongue in Chic* seeks to complement, not compete with these groups and without them, *TiC* wouldn't have happened.

I was an occasional poet. I wrote poems mostly for my own amusement and, when asked to, for special occasions. I hit one of those elusive seams of inspiration and wrote six or seven in a week and sent them in to Monkey Kettle, the local poetry and other stuff magazine published as a labour of love by matthew michael taylor and a team of dedicated friends. (I assume they're friends. For all I know they might hate each other's guts and have overcome their differences for the sake of Art, but one doesn't like to pry).

matthew made encouraging sounds and published two poems and I was delighted. He then introduced me to "Poetry Kapow". <KAPOW!> (It's a local thing – those of you old enough to remember "Crackerjack" may understand). So it was I called myself a poet for the first time in public on 2 May, 2008. Here I met the wonderful Fay and Danni who stage marvellously eclectic events grounded in Performance Poetry. I'm not unfamiliar with taking a stage or a Mic, but I physically shook during my five minutes Open Mic spot. The audience was very supportive; laughed in all the right places and gave me a rousing reception. Someone even shouted out "You rock". This was the first time it was aimed at me without a heavy dose of irony. My terror subsided after that and I enjoyed the range of writers, music and inter-active art installations on display.

Kapow! gave me a taste for performing poetry and led to an appearance at the local festival, "Stony Live". After that I hit the internet and looked for other events that offered Open Mic opportunities. There weren't many close

A Brief History of Rhyme

to Milton Keynes so I started to travel. I next went to Poetry Bites at Kings Heath in Birmingham and then I read about something called "Slams" (Poets perform their poetry in three minute slots and judges from the audience decide the winner). I went to my first one with Farrago in London. This was what I call my "Light Bulb Moment".

There was an excellent line up of featured poets and I found myself sitting with Graham Frost, an independent Radio Producer and Dr Stewart, both of whom work on *"Bespoken Word"* for Radio 4. They kindly cheered for me when it was my turn to slam. I finished as a runner up in a wonderful night. This was when I started to think "Why do I have to travel fifty miles to see quality guests and address an audience on a regular basis? Why can't Milton Keynes (population 230,000) have their own event?" So I started planning. The key ingredient for me would be to bring in guest poets to showcase their talent and inspire local writers.

I made enquiries; undertook research; sent out emails; called a meeting in a pub which a dozen promised to attend but only five did. Lots of positive noises were made and offers of support came (the website was born, generously and ably supplied by Ian Barker) but most people already had a full calendar of family, work and other artistic commitments. It was around this time I received a text saying (I paraphrase here but not by much) "I don't want to piss on your parade but expect apathy. We've tried all this before and lost money every time. We've never received funding so be prepared for disappointment". I hate to think of the text I would have received if they HAD wanted to piss on my parade! Being something of a stubborn ass, this made me determined to give things a go. Surely it's better to try and fail than not try at all?

I booked the wonderful MADCAP as a venue who did me a deal. AF Harrold agreed to be our guest for a small fee, knowing we were trying to get something off the ground. A friend designed a flyer for free and

A Brief History of Rhyme

someone printed them at cost. Off I went in search of an audience. As a new venture unlike anything else in Milton Keynes, local paper *MK Citizen* gave us a nice piece in the Arts section. However in advance of the first gig on 11 January, 2009 I had precisely zero bookings or reservations for tickets. I started to panic. To make myself feel better I wrote out envelopes with the names of people who had said they would come. This came to about thirty. That was a decent start I felt and made me feel better. I was committed to expenditure of about £200 for the night with only £100 to come in ticket sales (if those thirty actually turned up). I was also committed to a follow up event in March. If things didn't take off, I could quietly close the thing down with a manageable loss I would put down to experience.

The launch night came and we put forty chairs out, generously spaced to make the room look full and close to the start time, they filled up. We put out ten more. They filled up. We put ten more out and they filled up with no room for any more. People stood round the edges and at the bar. Seventy souls (God bless every one of you!) came to witness the birth of the latest cultural New Kid on the Block and TWENTY FOUR poets signed up to read.

The audience seemed to be in top gear from the very first minute and, in short, it was an amazing evening. AF was superb and the audience went for his wonderful poetry in a big way. We managed to fit every reader in although we finished at 11pm. The audience bought merchandise, had a great time and mainly by accident, I had managed to recreate the buzz of the events that had inspired me at the first time of asking. I was on SUCH a high I didn't get much sleep that night. Best of all, I had covered my costs AND had £60 in the kitty for the next event.

We managed to attract some Arts Council funding and we booked two guests per event. Over the first year, *TiC* developed a reputation as a quality, professional, poetry event. The standard of Open Mic writing and performing

A Brief History of Rhyme

progressed and we formed a gang of bandit poets prepared to blag an Open Mic spot anywhere within fifty miles. Wonderful feedback came from the audience and guest performers earning the unsolicited testimonials:

"Pound for pound, the best poetry night in the Midlands"
Audience member

"A very special Poetry Sunday"
John Hegley

Within a year, *Tongue in Chic* went from nothing to a flourishing event with a planned anthology. So many thanks are due to many people (a list follows) and I am very grateful to Arts Council England and Arts Gateway MK for financial support.

However, my biggest thanks are due to the local writers, performers and audience. This is YOUR event and your talent, support and generosity of spirit has made the events so special. To all of you, thank you!

This anthology is essentially a Community project rather than an academic exercise. Poets who had taken part in the Tongue in Chic Open Mic sessions were invited to participate and no one was turned away. Most of our professional guest poets kindly agreed to contribute so you will find new writers nestling gently against John Hegley, Zena Edwards, Niall O'Sullivan, Paul Lyalls, AF Harrold, Rachel Pantecnicon, Liz Bentley and Richard Tyrone Jones. I've been amazed at the output of our local poets and I'm proud to share them with you.

Mark Niel
Tongue in Chic

Heartfelt thanks and appreciation go to...

matthew michael taylor

Fay Roberts

Danni Kushner

Ian Barker

Richard Frost

Steve Hobbs

Carolyn and Tony at MADCAP

David Lovesy

Denise Niel

AF Harrold

Sammy Jones

Keiren Phelan

Lucy Bedford

Steve Allen

Jacqui Rowe

Denise Niel

Rachel Pantechnicon

John Paul O'Neill

Tony Stringfellow

Russell Thompson

Niall O'Sullivan

Liz Bentley

Sean Kelly

Craig Lambert

John Stammers

Sarah Duran

Denise Niel

Richard Tyrone Jones

John Hegley

Yaw Asiyama

Marcus Moore

Sara Jane Arbury

Denise Niel

Steve Larkin

Zena Edwards

Laura King

Mac McFadden

Paul Lyalls

Simon Munnery

Peter Hunter

Luke Ashmead

Denise Niel

Peter Wyton

Guy Russell

Judi Moore

Steve Clark

Justin Thyme

Peter Ebsworth

Sharon Clark

BBC Three Counties Radio

Arts Council England

Arts Gateway MK

and finally... Denise Niel: for letting me, be me.

Steve Allen

Steve Allen's poetic themes are love with a sensitive touch, travel with a warped humour twist, and a penchant for the risqué.

A top-of-the-bill performance generated this newspaper review, "for excitement, check Steve Allen – he can give an audience a slow orgasm with his witty sexual verbosity!"

He was one of 500 contestants in 'MK Factor', a trial-by-jury competition to find the best of the town's performing arts. Waving the flag for what he calls "LOUD poetry from Milton Keynes", Steve was successful, the only poet awarded a gig as part of the town's 40th birthday celebrations.

Away from the realm of poetry, Steve has entered the thespian world, taking stage roles and co-writing pantomime scripts. And in *The Bedfordshire Clanger*', a short film, he played a vicar, which he claims makes up for the sexual verbosity. Hmm …

In 2009, Steve was a winner in Indigo Dreams Summer Collection competition. The prize is publication of his first collection, *Tasting The Fruit*'.

Steve Allen

NESTING

The billowing pillow of white
hosts a gash of orange,
a smothering mother
guarding a cache.

Further along,
the smaller hoard
of the moorhen.

And now,
another two canoodling bipeds,
wingless,
break at the sound
of my footfall.

Eggs fertilise,
cell divides,
powered by two.

TAMARIND

At one of Rio's many juice bars,
I ask for suco de tamarindo sem açucar,
because I want to taste the fruit
not the sweetener.

In bed with you,
I wish for the day you'll accept sexo sem preservativo,
because I want to feel the woman
not the sheath.

Steve Allen

DOUBLES ENTENDRES

First game, first set,
evenly matched.
As she stretches for the ball,
he sweats at the tight opening.

"Advantage me", he forecasts.
But no,
her contact is perfect.
Love one.

She's ready for the next.
"New balls please."
Later, singles over,
"fancy doubles?"

So long as it's good sets.

PLUG AND PLAY

She fingers the box,
finds a way in.
Well packed, but she
eases the contents out.
Easily turned on,
visibly ready to use.

Selects virus protection,
preventing infection
while sites are surfed,
safely.

Finds the hot spot.
At this rate,
download won't be long.

Steve Allen

TESSELLATION

Leaving at the end
of an over-extended stay,
she missed the true meaning of
"the house will be empty without you".

EARLY RETIREMENT

I retired early,
but then I took early retirement,
and now I go to bed late.

OCCUPATIONAL HAZARDS

Indian lorry drivers survive on opium
bought easily at truckstops.
But their lives are not so easy:
98% have high blood pressure,
earned alongside the bonus
for delivering perishable goods
from Calcutta to Delhi.

And our taxi driver balances the wheel
as he squeezes limestone powder paste
from a tube and mixes it with tobacco,
to freshen himself.
Later he opens his door and spits, on the move.
Perhaps, "on three", we passengers should emulate this?

At Jaisalmer fort,
medieval life plays out before us.
Every house is a shop,
cows and pigs meander,
and the female shit-shoveller cleans up.

Steve Allen

UNPICKED

School cricket captains pick, pick, pick,
and whittle down to the belittled,
the remains,
the rump.
Me.

Opposition injury creates imbalance.
Five uncomfortable years,
as the failure in sport,
the obvious transfer.
Me.

Slipped into the slips,
I stand horrified.
First ball,
second ball.

Third ball nicked,
rises slightly,
drops lightly.

I offer two unexpecting hands.
It lands, it stays.
A dolly catch.

Batsman horrified.
Disgraced at being caught by
me.

Alan Bainbridge

Alan lives in Milton Keynes and Sarlat La Caneda in France. He started life as a mathematician – it's been a long road.

He writes poetry because he has to:

"Art is a way of entering the world"
This bloke was saying on a TV program;
And it's true -
      We live so much inside ourselves;
      We need a door to freedom.

Alan Bainbridge

WANTING

The mind is overwhelmed;
And then the sadness comes;
Its inability to comprehend;
How this glorious vastness turns.
Observe a petal, its perfect curvature;
The way it cups, its fine lined artistry;
Feel its cool, soft, sensual texture;
And those colours – shaded to sublime degree.
Imbibe its perfume's heady strong infusion;
Allow the almost physical intrusion;
Its recollecting and transporting power:
So nearly bliss,
    Unreached, just missed;
    To know all this –
Yet still not see the flower!

INTROSPECTION

I know
the I that I know knows
but does this I know
that that I knows
this I?
Is the I I know I
or the I that knows
I know I?
Or am I us?
Are we?

Alan Bainbridge

LOSS

The sky is rent.
Oh the Earth still blooms;
My garden's grass cut scent;
But the sky is ripped like doom.
And yonder where I avert my stare;
The loud thunder of tumultuous atmosphere;
Assures in shrieks of lightning fright;
That the planet still behaves aright.
The crowd still mulls as if it does not see.
Their busy work, and fights for centre stage!
An old woman eyes damp with the patina of age;
Talks of "our Joe", "his Jill", "their Betty".
And of course I join in;
Not to seem impolite, or worse impolitic.
Is this how we are taken in?
On graves our graceless frolic!
(The old woman, knows the path;
And simply looks and laughs.)
Sometimes, when I can summon up the courage;
I look at it square on;
And run my fingers round its gentle jagged edge;
And try to love it as I love the Moon.
But it won't do!
This insult sets my world awry;
This star filled blackness in the bright noon day;
Is ugly;
And it's here to stay.

Alan Bainbridge

THERE IS AN AGE

There is an age,
Vaguely suspected,
An age of hilltops and broad vistas;
Somewhat lonely,
(There is less space up here)
A reassuring nod across the valley;
The occasional visitors;
Who shake their heads;
On the way back down;
To join the thousands who,
 "At his bidding speed;
And post o'er land and ocean without rest";
While you, now more discerning, ask:
"Who's bidding?"

You mind the weather less;
There is still a hunkering down;
But more and more, you simply are;
And are consciousness;
There is the night sky;
And sunshine;
The river winding out of view;
A half remembered tune,
Or lost refrain;
And there the greatest sadness is:
To know that soon;
This will all be gone;
Like tears in the rain.

David Baker david@davidbakerdesign.co.uk ~ +44 (0)7912 842682

David grew up a disturbed child with an irrational fear of poets – this was mainly due to his Grandpa telling him that Robert Frost had sucked the breath from all of David's Gran's family members during a particulalry eventful Whitsun. The *fear* did not improve during the 1970s. David could often be seen running away from his parents' house during Sunday evenings, whilst *'That's Life'* was entertaining the nation, with both fists clenched, screaming: "Cyril Fletcher, you bastard. Keep away from my mouth!" Sadly, Pam Ayres proved equally unpopular with something faintly demonic beneath her visage.

Since those troubled times David has left the poets behind and made a career as a creative (dis)assembler, or 'sticker-down', of other people's words, design briefs and mission statements – working in such famous places as London, Amsterdam and Luton. Occasionally, but sadly not this time, he is allowed to use some pictures and some colours to fill in bits near the edges.

David quite mistakenly believes that working and helping on such a worthwhile, creative arts-based local project, far from his comfort zone, will bring him to the attention of local businesses who are seeking to build creative partnerships with a local, independent, senior design creative who currently works on multi-lingual design projects for The Tata Group (Corus Steel), Pilkington Glass/NSG Group and Swiss fragrance company Givaudan. David has also created and maintained corporate identities for management group GLCE Ltd and a collective of London auction houses, antiques dealers and fine art galleries – KCSADA.

So, in the spirit of rapprochement, David has chosen the following critique:

Poets have been mysteriously silent on the subject of cheese.

G.K. Chesterton

Ian Barker

This prolific "oversized poet" now lives in Omaha, Nebraska where he confuses his neighbours by pronouncing everything "with a pretty accent", pointing out he is originally British not Australian and freaking out the local librarian by making the only request in living memory for a complete set of e. e. cummings and Kerouac anthologies. He has spent considerable time teaching fellow Americans how to make proper tea: hot, the colour of wood, no sugar and definitely no ice.

You can read more of his work and get in touch at www.alexsykie.com

Ian Barker

EXPRESSION

For my mother, who liked their art but not their implementation.
For my father, who cried at The Sleeper and was proud of me for being his son.
For my sister, who may never understand them though they brought a lump to her throat.
For my nephew, who I hope will one day see the gods do not all play for Manchester United.
For my lover, who shines from within.
For my past, which sinned against me as I sinned against it.
For my future, however short, or long; I hope I use you well.
For atonement.

DO NOT VENERATE THE PLACE.

Do not venerate the place.
It is passive and did not write the songs
and knew no clever rhymes nor mastered
meter with the well-placed feet that you so admire.

The event was a magnificent fleeting sliver of time
that bloomed in our past and grew in our
unintended lying to fit a need,
way beyond the deed.

You set it on an altar with signs and guides
and glass cabinets;
but the goodness of the moment, the worth
of the story, is long gone.
Gone in reality, passed. Living on
in your words which are a distorted
lense that bends the light of the truth
so it curves to fit your purposes,
however well intentioned.

Ian Barker

Do not venerate the place, do not
make it an undeserving monument where white-gloved
curators must tremble at an imagined
majesty and handle the crumbs of our
everyday tables with a breath-holding
reverence, heavy to the touch with
import and meaning which they agonise
over obsessed and
are tested so that they may say
they have a certificate that signifies
their understanding of what we were and
what we stood for in every way.

We lived here in ordinary ways. We made all
our mistakes, fallible and room-spinning,
puking, with a depth only you see and we wished
we had in our time. Your artifacts were our broken clay pipes
and your big discoveries were the rotting bones of our dogs.
So, do not venerate the place; lay down the next generation of
legend and trails with your own flints and sonnets.

CAKES AND INSECTS

At the start of it all the Chef made a cake.
He put in a filling, of jam and cream,
warmed up his big Chef oven
and the cake began to bake.

Placed on the side, left to cool,
insects crawled over it, had insect fights,
lived strong, happy lives,
no wars,
some battles, more like struggles,
but they served a purpose although the insects
did not know it,
and even the Chef would not have been sure.
Chef came along,
added some icing, pink and white,
sugary, nice,

Ian Barker

made it perfect, glossed it over,
shone it like ice.
Chef added candles, a border, of green,
little stick people with little stick dogs and cats
with little stick houses slightly better than shacks.

The insects stole icing, crumbs and bits
and built themselves up stronger, became smarter,
learned tricks.
Insects had parties, brought bottles,
got lost.
Loved one another, sung songs,
wrote books.

Chef lit the candles, 12 sparkly lights,
upsetting the insects,
who had 'intelligent' fights and debated
the meaning of candle lighting, into the night.

Insects planned rebellions, hoarded cake,
built fences.
To ensure cake protection; raised strong defences.
Insect life got more complicated,
and took on more 'dimensions'.

Then someone ate the cake.

The insects learned to live on the crumbs left
behind on the table.
Lived weaker, deeper lives
and told tall stories of imagined crumbs
the size of an insect house.

Until there were no crumbs left.

And the insects died.

And not even the Chef cried.

Ian Barker

And the table carried on being a table
even though the insects were dead,
and the cake was gone,
(all the candles were out and in the bin).

The Chef made another mixture,
mixed it up and made it shaped like a cake.
He warmed up the oven,
and put it in to bake.

LUMP
For the runners and those who lost the race...

This is the reality worm that spits on your breakfast so you lose your appetite.

This is the hitch-hiker who steals your dreams whilst you sleep, scribbles out days
on your calendar and adjusts your priorities without asking if it's ok.

This is the bringer of a vain hope that God exists, or that at least love really can
conquer all, despite the odds.

This is someone else's epic battle that you've read about and it loomed
unplanned on your horizon whilst you are still Far Too Young and have So Many
Things Left To Do.

This is the teacher of new words, new statistics and new ways of saying things,
like "whipple" and "procedure" and "chances" and "affairs in order".

This is the pink ribbon and the races in memory of you.

This is how you get to be yesterday's face in a photograph.

This....is....IT.

Fight IT. Don't give up.

Ian Barker

IMPACT

When I die I want to have made an impact.
Not the kind that arises from close meteor contact.
Or that sort which you get when performing the half stock-broker with double twist from the
top of the nearest skyscraper. I'm less desperate than that.

It's not enough to have littered the world with progeny who didn't take my name, although it's a shame. I'm not bothered by the fruits of my labour –
they'll wash away soon enough,
on the next technological tidal wave – I only did it for the money; I did it grumpily and for financial gain.

There are no cocktails named in my honour.
No twists or slings or things mixed two parts gin.
No sex-on-the-beach brain-cell stunner.
No exotic fruits or names with Latin woven in to defeat the brains of spliffy students in their final summer.

They'll bury me nicely and read Dylan Thomas poems at my eulogy. There will be flowers, for a generation, but eventually neglect will come to stake its claim.
Nobody will be remembered enough to blame.

In time, my skin will putrefy and decompose and my best burial clothes will unravel around worms who'll wriggle through my eye sockets and romp with partying beetles who'll munch on my crusty bits and nest in my pockets.

In years to come, when the creepy crawly disco is done:
When the mound above me has sunk and the veneration stone at my head has greened with the lichen of a second generation of dead –
who will know I had a clean driving licence and paid all my taxes on time?

Liz Bentley

Liz Bentley is a writer, poet, comedienne, host, programmer, musician, mother, therapist and insomniac. She has been working on the performance poetry/cabaret/comedy circuit for 7 years with her Casio keyboard and ukulele.

Since winning Short Fuse Poetry Idol and later Poetry Idol the Rivals in 2003, Liz's performance has gone from strength to strength and she has been programmed at events such as Latitude Festival, Alternative Village Fete (National Theatre) and the Ledbury Poetry Festival. Liz has taken three shows to the Edinburgh Fringe. Liz also works as a therapist. Her experiences of therapy and having a diagnosis of multiple sclerosis have taken her into disability arts

"Definitely one of my Fringe highlights" Three Weeks *****

"Like a female Ivor Cutler" The Scotsman

"Bentley is beguiling. Such an exhilarating experience" Chortle

www.lizbentley.co.uk/

Liz Bentley

PLANTING BULBS

I've been buying lampshades
Quite expensive too
But when I got them home today
The tag on the lampshades read –
"No more than 60 watt light bulbs in us please."
I took an interest in lampshades because I recently won (in my housing
associations quarterly magazine competition) one hundred 100watt light bulbs
I will now plant the light bulbs and the squirrels can have them
Or I'll break them up before I plant them and the squirrels will choke on them
Serves them right for messing with my daffodil bulbs

SWIMMING WITH JEREMY IRONS

I was at the Peckham Pulse swimming baths when I noticed a man who looked
just like Jim Morrison
I swam a little closer, he didn't look quite so much like Jim Morrison, but never
the less I thought I would tell him that I'd just swallowed some water, thinking
that he would then link this – to then thinking that I would swallow his come
I would then acknowledge his thoughts and tell him that I don't do swallowing
come unless it's completely necessary like, for example, I was being raped and if I
didn't do it I'd die –or I'd been on a desert island for days and was really thirsty.
After that, I'd report him to the lifeguard who would expel him from the centre
and he'd have to go to Wavelengths in Deptford.
When you get up close to the lifeguard he looks just like Jeremy Irons' twin
brother

Liz Bentley

THANK YOU UNIVERSE

Thank you universe for those beautiful hand embroidered pictures that auntie Brenda made last Christmas that I forgot to thank her for.

Thank you universe for our times of celebration, Christmas, New Year, Easter, Divali, all those wonderful bank holidays when we get together with our families. Thank you for the happiness and great joy it brings to us all.

Thank you universe for the amazing gift of life, Jesus's life, Jeremy Iron's life – all life. Thank you to my mother and father for bringing me into this life.

Thank you for the wonderful education I had, without which, I wouldn't have been told recently how unique my ignorance is.

Thank you for the joy of love, sex and sexually transmitted diseases that gave my sister and I something in common.

Thank you for my boyfriend Mark Sidnell for not walking me home from the pub on 29th July 1981 so that Janet Bloomfield could beat me up in confidence so I will never forget the date when Charles and Diana got married which often comes up in pub quizzes.

Thank you Auntie Brenda for never taking me to France like you promised because I eventually went to Paris via the Channel tunnel instead of a crappy old boat trip to Calais

Thank you princess Diana for dying on 31st August 1997 and making my day trip to Paris so much more exciting and memorable and making me want to thank Auntie Brenda even more.

Thank you Janet Bloomfield for apologizing for beating me up because you got the wrong person and thank you to my mother for giving me her passive-aggressive genes so I would forgive Janet Bloomfield but suppress my anger that then made my legs numb and my eyes blurred.

Liz Bentley

Thank you Dr Bari for diagnosing these symptoms as multiple sclerosis, without which I would not be driving my brand new motorbility Vauxhall Zafira 2.2 with air conditioning and power steering, complete with the blue badge for parking, the freedom pass and exemption from the congestion charge.

Thank you Ronald McDonald for providing me with soft white toilet paper for all the years I was unemployed and thank you Ronald McDonald for putting locks on your toilet roll holders, giving me the incentive to look for a job.

Thank you to my old flute teacher Mr Long (a short man who abused me at school), without him I would never have gone into therapy, psychoanalysed my MS symptoms away and found a career in therapy and thank you to all the other Mr Longs out there who keep me in employment.

And lastly, thank you universe for the Rasta Father Christmas's that can occasionally be seen inside a whole peanut if you look really closely.

Liz Bentley

SUMMER IS A COMING

I want to go to a fete
I need to go to a fete
The only place where I can buy a crochet toilet roll holder
And I need one urgently
Because my relationship is so dysfunctional that we're thinking about moving to
the country and opening up a bed and breakfast

SUMMER IS A COMING

Lets get down to the carnival and watch the floats
We'll get free sweets chucked out from the cat neuter project
Birdseed from the Montessori nurseries
And pencils from the Free Masons
"Oh, roll it up in a pencil," said the therapist to the sex offender
When it gets dark, chill out time, but be careful of the three-legged greyhounds
when the fireworks go off
Then, condom wrappers, slice your foot open on broken glass and put your tent
up – free camping – they'll think you're drying it out
Have a fire and baked bean cans explode, embers shoot into the tent, scarring
you for life.

Liz Bentley

JOB INTERVIEW

Dear Madam,

Re: Sexual health services and advice for young people — post of counselling supervisor

Thank you for your letter dated 28th September informing me of my unsuccessful interview.

Obviously, on paper, I am extremely qualified for this position. Otherwise there would have been no interview. But, unfortunately, I had a gig the night before and it was free beer and a very late night. I may well have appeared stoned, but I would like to put you in the picture, that that's just the breastfeeding and lack of sleep — no drugs were taken on this occasion.

I was indeed nervous when I arrived at your centre, I am usually good at switching roles from comedienne to therapist, but you guys just caught me out. I apologize for calling your professionals 'you guys,' and when you asked how I felt about abortion, what could I say? I know so much about the subject I thought you would have read my mind and/or my CV and I could only throw my hands up and say, 'Abortion. Whey....'

I look forward to receiving your feedback.

Yours sincerely,

Liz Bentley

Tim Dalgleish

Born, Houghton Regis, 1966. I've studied Philosophy, Film and the Holocaust at the universities of North London, London, New York, The Open University, the British Film Institute and the British Language Centre in Madrid. I've various teaching qualifications but enjoyed most teaching evening classes in Philosophy.

Acted professionally for RAT Theatre Company and was deeply involved in amateur theatre for years especially with Bare Bones Theatre Company. The past decade developed a passion for Spain, documentary filmmaking and once again poetry. Recently, I've performed (badly!) poems at *Tongue in Chic* and had a couple of poems in Monkey Kettle poetry magazine.

Publications:

Plays
Stride, a musical, (1985).
The Collector, adapted John Fowles novel, co-written with Caz Tricks, (1998).
Pigshit: The Life and Theatre of Antonin Artaud, (1999).

Non-fiction books
The Guerilla Philosopher: Colin Wilson and Existentialism, (1993).
Lifting It Off The Page: 25 Oral Portraits of OU People, (1994).

Tim Dalgleish

PLUMS

Fated, on the day of rest, to feel the insignificance of God's day and idle
With inconsiderate noisiness, I was throwing stones at the windows of a widow.
In the mouth a sweet taste of plums stolen from her garden.
God's infinite temper, no doubt, filling the aether, making the plums
Just a touch redder and purpler than nature would have rendered.
She the schoolteacher, so small children had had their heads filled,
By her schoolish thoughts, her face, like their heads
Now, no longer a tabula rasa, weariness of insistent clamouring...
Unhappily she wrote, 'Dorothy Parker Appreciates Art':
Men are pigs that love/ With pen and ink/ Their faces blank/
White valentines/ Never writing what/ They goddam think/
But/ Trotting off when/ They see the signs/
'She aint no lady/
About to faint
' /But/ Drafting letters/ To boys that paint.
...Voices, had spoken crow's feet around the eyes, spat,
Indentations upon her chin, riven loud grooves upon her brow.
So a certain life persisted in her eyes, while mine were glazing,
No reply being made, the sun so hot and I recreating Hieronymous
Bosch in my head, I heard a voice from within, 'Come in'.
Turned the handle, climbed the stair, each step, a picture:
Icarus-
Falls-Brueghel-steps-in-blood-Dali-cuts-tuna-steps-scarlet-as-a-lie
Every madness, she had felt, expressed, her time, at school, expelled.
I went in, she was lying, head half covered by an idle arm.
She was lying, crying gently, our hour passed, words no consolation
And I had fallen, as silent as the silent graves one could see,
From her window, coal black birds sitting and soaring high above
The short plum trees.
Tears felt strange,
With her face,
Her fate,
Her eyes,
As black and red as the plums.
Fated, on the day of rest, to feel the insignificance of God's day and idle
With inconsiderate noisiness, I was throwing stones at the windows of a widow.

Tim Dalgleish

A GALA DAY IN THE EIGHTEENTH CENTURY

The Gala Day is about the sun blessed land,
A rope's strung up by a steady, stoic hand.
A gaggle of children run about and sing,
For they guess not, what darkness a day can bring.
An old man with grinning beard like Bernard Shaw,
Will cheer his crook-nosed son who upholds this law.
Broiling adults winnow in the market place,
Soon to choose the choicest multi-coloured face.
It is as if the village is up in arms,
But Lord, their hoarse voices sing not battle psalms.
Only foul melodies, ditties, mixed in gin,
Out drowning their children before they begin.
All the nation it will bellow heady praise
As silent offenders sink and voices raise.
I wonder if the poor, breathless, beggars aren't,
Just murdered for want of a magistrates slant?
Henry Fielding, he will form the force of Bow,
Carried on by blind John to defeat the low.
But for now the mighty Tyburn tree holds strong,
And Laughing Jack draws a trembling, thirsty throng.
On public Gala Days they 'pulled a leg' with mirth,
Exhausted breath with angled beam, knotted girth.
Gala is 'Gallows' in Anglo-Saxon tongue,
And once, on two syllables, many thousands,
Hung.

Tim Dalgleish

AND, STILL

I have lived my life in fragments,
Tossed into the road, crushed under boot by better days.
They lay like sodden wintered leaves, pell-mell.
And I cannot sweep them up, tidy or focus them into neat new piles.
I have lived life in fragments.
Days together have become
One, moment, an hour, a year has become, a forgotten revolution.
Photographic evidence colours my misty memoir, my blue remembered hill.
My lover sitting still and still and still,
Life has been fragmented for I,
Want nothing better than to see the road,
In all its glory.
But the journey's path, a weary walk, to nowhereness,
Seems strange underfoot, but maybe yes,
I can see in mist,
The fragments of life that have been lived.
Drifted, turned, bumbled.
Perhaps have been whole,
Feeling fragmented.
My life,
A leaf, a book, a path,
A gutter,
A stutter,
A murmur
Not so, but so, and so, and in the wind, the fragments fly
To settle,
One upon the other,
Perhaps, a single
Place time
In.

Tim Dalgleish

HOMENAJE

Lisboa eres tan simple como el mar,
Profundo, vago, luminoso, sereno, gentil,
Tienes olas de especias, calles de musica,
Lisboa eres elegante como tu poeta.
Pessoa eres verde como el vino de tu mente,
Tienes palabras y rostros ampliados,
Pessoa eres una hoja blanca,
Como una voz en el aire de crystal.
Lisboa y pessoa eran tan simples como el mar,
Fresco, emocionado, lleno, magnifico,
Hasta el cofre esta vacio,
Y te metes en las calles de Aflama.
Como en una gran bibliotheca de caras y nombres,
Tu claridad se apaga, ausente, arrullando,
Y otra vez vuele a ser una mano desnuda.

Translation of Homenaje:
Lisbon you are as simple as the sea,/ Profound, vast, luminous, serene, gentle,/
You have waves of spices, streets of music, /Lisbon you are elegant like your
poet.// Pessoa you are green as the wine of your mind,/ Your words are deep
your faces broad,/ Pessoa you are a blank page (leaf),/ Like a voice in the crystal
air.//
Lisbon and Pessoa they are simple as the sea,/ Fresh, emotional, full,
magnificent,/ Until the trunk is empty,/ And you withdraw into the steets of the
Alfama.//
As a great library of faces and names,/ Your clear light dims, absent, lulling,/And
becomes once again a naked hand.

Tim Dalgleish

THE NATIONAL GALLERY: ARGENTINE SCULPTURES, GREEK THOUGHTS

Scullptures of the mental heart,
Stand.
St Sebastian kneels, carved by arrows,
Whose heads are lost, in flesh,
Standing,
Lost in thought,
One torturer, pulls the cord, we cannot see,
The black hood, dark and hot, obscures his contemplation.
This marriage of burnt wood, for hair,
Paint wash and onyx eye, with the moving stillness
Of the sculptor's art,
Is like a chisel in the flesh,
A brush with death,
A rock in the hand,
Whilst we stand.
At a stoning.
'Here' said Parmenides 'are the gates of the paths of Night and Day':
There are two roots around the sword of humanity,
One submission,
To omit the other.
They both sink deep to the heart.
There are two buds heavy growing in humanity,
One thought,
To act the other.
Devotion to both cradles parent and child.
There are two roses pinned to the tears of humanity,
One petal pale,
The other dappled dark.
Our wedding is a bed of roses.
There are two paths deep red across the garden of life,
One of flowers
One of thorns.
Both paths of pain but distinctive in their scent.

Rex De'Ath-Vale

Rex wrote this poem when he was 9 years old and the poem was passed round all his teachers in the staff room at his middle school as his literacy teacher was so impressed with it.

Rex has written a few poems and the occasional song during his younger years and continues to write short stories.

Rex is now 14 and likes cats, cars, computer games, crafts, karting and cooking cakes!

Rex De'Ath-Vale

THE BANANA SKIN

A banana lay in a sack.
He was torn, shredded and peeled and ripped.
Soon he would be gone forever.
He didn't like to be this way.
He lay there and thought back to.
Back to when he was in the hands of a man.
When he was raised to the mouth
And about to be eaten by him.
His red tongue moving with hunger.
He didn't like to be this way.
He lay there and thought back to.
Back to when he fell in the fruit bowl in fear,
With oranges, kiwis and apples.
Three weeks he was there.
He didn't like to be this way.
He lay there and thought back to.
Back to when he was carried in a truck
With thousands of other bananas too.
On a boat. The boat was moving,
Moving too slowly for them to slide.
He didn't like to be this way.
He lay there and thought back to.
Back to when he was on his tree, happy.
Hanging with apples and kiwi fruit
And others like himself. In the steaming sun.
And feeling the breeze on his skin.

Paul Eccentric

Paul is a performance poet, playwright, singer and novelist, based in Aston Clinton. Bucks.

He is one half of The Antipoet, who have been storming the circuit throughout the year, through the RRRANTS Collective. His play, 'The Sorry People' toured England culminating in a rave Edinburgh Festival finale. His cartoon, *'The Immortal Henri Blutoe'* premiered in Covent Garden in October and can be found on Youtube. His latest collection of poetry, *'The Kult of the Kazoo'*, was published last year by RRRANTS.

www.pauleccentric.co.uk   www.rrrants.com

Paul Eccentric

PUBLIC CONVENIENCE

It's convenient for you
to keep me angry,
just like a cobra being baited
with a stick,
as while I focus my attention
on placebos
I'll miss the sleight of hand
of your next trick.
You create the need for me
to work much faster,
then try to slow me down
with cameras and laws,
and works designed for
maximum frustration,
while your sly manoeuvres
everyone ignores.
You shift the blame
for all your bald deceptions;
you demonise the innocent,
and hide,
behind the blind of benign
benefactor,
your lies disguised as
nationalistic pride.
You'd like to keep me scared
as much as angry,
convinced my way of life
is under threat,
but the greatest enemy
to things I value
are the freedoms
you conveniently forget!

Paul Eccentric

'1420 Mhz'

He wrote a single word in the margin.
One word.
Three letters and an exclamation mark.
'Wow!'
And it seemed so inadequate for the sentiment that he wanted to express.
'Wow!'~
a word coined to convey the feeling of profound exclamation.
For that was how he felt as his mind struggled to digest the information in front of him.
Just 'Wow!'
'Is there anybody out there?' he had asked, as people had been asking since time immemorial, can anybody hear me?
Is there anyone listening in the wider galaxy?'
'Are we alone; are we unique, as the world's religions preach or merely pebbles on sentience beach?'
To know the answers to these questions would be.....
Wow!
That would change everything!
To know that ours was not the only form of life in existence might just have humbled us into accepting our own less than significance;
drawn a veil over our reliance on religion and superstition;
heralded the dawn of a new era in human evolution.
He had sent a message:
a coded riddle.
He had sent it out into the unknown.
He had reasoned that any alien life with the intelligence to receive such a signal would also be capable of translating his message
and responding in like.
'Wow!'
To be able to commune with a species from another world. To drag humanity kicking and screaming from the parochial isms of a stagnating society and to be able to nudge it toward a future devoid of such arrogant piety.
'Wow!'

Paul Eccentric

1420Mhz was his message: the frequency at which hydrogen, the most common element in the universe, emits radiation.
A simple message. A pulse that merely asks:'do we understand one another?'
'Are we on the same wavelength?'

A simple 'wow' scribbled in the margin, a 'wow' as he sees the results of the test:
At 1420Mhz-a discernible narrowband pulse.
Received!
And understood.
'Yes we do'.
So, wow, yes, wow!
What else could he have written?
What better word was there?
His peers had agreed that there would be little room for debate, and that a signal received at 1420Mhz would be accepted as an attempt by persons extraterrestrial to communicate, as no natural phenomena could incidentally replicate,
the traits
of a wow result.
And yet...
this is a true story and the Wow! signal was received in 1977.
So where are our neighbours?
Where is our brave new future?
And did our hero ever receive a second signal at 1420 MHz?
We'll probably never know.
The telescope was dismantled shortly afterwards and the observatory flattened to make way for a golf course.
Wow!

Paul Eccentric

NOBODY'S HERO

Does anybody here know
what makes someone a hero?
Is it the bloke who kicks a
ball about on a Saturday afternoon?
Well, it would appear so,
but is it that clear, though?
Is it the girl with the silly
haircut who can bash out a
catchy tune?
And is letting your fear show
not an act for a hero?
Is it someone who loses their life
while fighting in evil and illegal
wars?
Does seeing their tears flow
make them less of a hero?
Or are heroes
just weirdoes
who talk up career lows
when really they're just
party bores?

Paul Eccentric

CHILD ON BOARD

Hello! How the devil are you?
It's been an absolute age!
Haven't seen you since... ooh, I
don't know when.
So where've you been, then?
What've you been up to since I
last saw you?
A baby? Really?
He can? Can he really?
Walking on his second day?
That's amazing.
Talking before he even left
the womb?
How marvellous!
But how are you in yourself,
though?
He never did.
Potty trained within a week?
Advising the government on fiscal
policy while still at nursery?
You must be so proud.
And how about you? Do you
still keep in touch with–
really?
Oxford before his fourth birthday?
Crikey.
Standing for parliament at five.
Is that allowed? They changed
the rules just for him.
Of course they did.
But you. My old friend.
What about YOU??

Paul Eccentric

How have-did he. I would have
expected no less.
The Nobel Peace Prize at six.
What can I say.
BUT WHAT ABOUT YOU?!
YOU. YOURSELF.
I know all about the kid.
I feel I was practically at
the birth!
What have YOU done since
I last saw you?
I mean, apart from having a
child genius?
Where have you been?
First man on Mars?
Really? Oh well, fair play
to you!

Zena Edwards

Zena Edwards is a poet and performer who uses song, movement and global influences as a jump-off for her words.

She defines the fusion of poetry and music by including traditional African-instrumentation (the Kalimba and Kora) and new technology, to create her own sound tracks for her poems and stories, producing a body of work that reaches culturally and generationally diverse audiences on an international level.

She has performed at Festivals worldwide and also works in schools and colleges, supported by the Apples and Snakes poetry organisation, 57 Productions and the British Council, and has shared the stage and anthologies with some of her most admired predecessors, Linton Kwesi Johnson, Sonia Sanchez, Lemn Sissay, Jean Binta Breeze and Roger McGough.

Zena Edwards

MARTHA'S DESCENT FROM THE PARK BENCH

More than perfect
Was Martha's descent from the park bench.
A magnificent aerial sprawling, a baboon squabble

of Elbows, twisting ankle, flailing head
angulated hip, contorted lip
To the shape of "Arrrgh ffuugfggrrshshhiiit!"

And her usually buoyant centre of gravity,
was taken by the charm
of the pull of moon and the earths magnetic dance,

she kaflumphed to the grass
a spasmodic arc, causing a minor tsunami in the Seychelles
all the contents of a bottle of vodka

once sloshing in her calves and heels
as if she waded through Friday night streets
in customized 4" galoshes

now find equilibrium, spirit level
in a horizontal status

coshed by 45% over proof
ah how she sleeps ?

Zena Edwards

NETWORK

The cat purrs licking itself clean
in the best chair in the house
The cooker time display lies. 2.37am really?

User ID:
Password:

"Hello Teresa "TT" Marshall!"
Status and mood question mark
What are you doing question mark
What's on your mind question mark

What's on your mind?

'Something brilliant, something brilliant!'
Myface network needs something brilliant and cool
'Something brilliant'
No less than blauw! blauw! spectacular for the Spacebook massive

What's on my mind... *Blank*

What's on your mind...? *Blank, blank*

       What's on your bloody mind? *Blank! Bloody blank!*

Like a space between.

WHAT IS ON YOUR MIND!!!
Is any-body-listening?'

She presses her nose
to the LCD screen
looking out into the world
licks it hard, watches
the liquid crystal scarper
then reconvene to scheme
her demise. No one to lick her clean
with a furry tongue

'Is any-body-listening?'

Zena Edwards

A REBELLIOUS THOUGHT

Neat corners, crusts cut off, nurse made beds
Clocking in, portioned time, compressed moments

every now and then
one will slip through
like a gamble, like a lie,
like a gas leak, like a liquid on the lung
adaptation, evolution

is there really escape or more means of self deception?
Caught up some where in the machine,
a nodule, a minute strip of copper
wishing it were free roaming mercury

Richard Frost

Richard Frost has been writing poetry on the quiet for many years, in the hope of remaining unrecognised in his own lifetime and perhaps being published posthumously in some ironic way. However, after going to an open mic night in January 2008 'just to watch', he was inspired to take his poetry off the page and onto the stage, and has since performed at many spoken word events across the East Midlands, London and the South East. A regular at *Tongue in Chic*, Richard is part of a collective of poets that aims to take performance poetry out to a wider audience within and beyond Milton Keynes.

Richard Frost

YAWN CHORUS

I always keep a yawn in a jar
Next to my bed for emergencies,
Along with a pile of old headaches;
I also have a small amount
Of shivers on my windowsill,
As bait to trap the dawn.
I hide my dreams under the pillow
With a bottle of fermented rainbows
And my door is always bolted shut
To keep the future out.
Sometimes I leave the curtains drawn
To let the shadows breed,
And often I am still awake
Long after the clock is asleep.

Richard Frost

HORSE

I wake early.
No alarm clock;
Just the Horse.
The cold dawn streets
Slide through liquid shades of grey;
Am I leading the Horse
Or is the Horse leading me?
At the bus stop the Horse grows impatient;
Presently others, each with their own Horse,
Arrive, and together we wait in our livery.
Checking watches, shivering into newspapers,
Champing at the bit until the bus comes, and then
The frantic surge as everyone tries
To be the first to get their Horse on board.
It makes me laugh;
Why do we relentlessly drag our Horses
Through these unnatural fields?
Is it to give them a sense of purpose?
They seem reluctant to me.
I think about what my father always said:
"It's the first thirty years that's the hardest
And the next twenty years are the worst."
His Horse is an old grey nag now;
Why doesn't he put it out to graze?
I know why.
I feel the same way
About my own Horse;
Every day I want to shoot it,
But I wouldn't let anyone
Take it away from me.

Richard Frost

THE COUNTRY OF THE BLIND

In the Country of the Blind
The One-Eyed Man is cursed
With visions of a world that
No-one else believes in,
And is thought to be delusional,
A liar, or insane,
When he tries to describe things like
Colours, reflections or shadows –
Things they don't even have words for.
He's derided for his nonsense talk
Of rainbows and sunsets,
And his claims about the moon and stars
Floating silently through the night sky
Remain impossible to prove either way.
He is regarded with the same unease
That we reserve for those who claim
To hear voices, talk with the dead,
Or travel on UFO's.
Yet worse for him is being condemned
To live with the daily horror of knowing
What shows on people's faces when
They think no-one is looking.

Richard Frost

STILL LIFE

Is this still life?
The clock weeps on –
Seconds stagger down its face
And drip from its lips like curses.

Is this still life?
The clock weeps on.
Is this still life?

The clock is growing anxious –
Its heart takes a beating
And races like time.
It strikes out with its hands
Screaming through broken glass jaws –
The years roll down its face
And drip from its lips like curses.

Is this still life?
The clock weeps on.

AF Harrold

AF Harrold is a somewhat popular English poet and performer.

AF Harrold

IN THE BEGINNING WAS THE LETTER

I can hardly think of anything better
than reading a letter
that's sent to the wrong address
although I don't mean to suggest
that I'd pry or snoop or open it up
but the paper knife slipped as I reached for a cup
and it's only polite
and morally right
to check that the name on the letter inside
doesn't live in the house where the letter's arrived
'cause sometimes, you know, mistakes are made –
envelopes get switched or the ink can fade
and a 37 Malborough Square
can look, through the haze of the breakfaster's hair,
like a 39 Pig Lane
and there's no one to blame
but when I looked closer and checked this one out
there wasn't a doubt
and it wasn't for us
and so I told Harry who made a small fuss
as he read it through twice
even the parts that weren't very nice and mentioned the vice
that a certain Julianne-May MacGuire
committed while posing nude with a lyre
and something she does on page four of the letter,
which I am sure, in time, could possibly get her
rewarded in Greece,
would make our police
take a very dim view,
especially since it took place in a pew,

AF Harrold

but I said to Harry and he said to me
that it was nothing compared to what on page three
happens to someone referred to as 'John'
and someone called Jim and also Yvonne
and a man who seems to be known just as 'X'
and someone called Jean, of indeterminate sex,
but then Harry held up the penultimate page
and waved it around as if in a rage
but he wasn't that angry, he just needed a biscuit,
so I handed him one, I thought that I'd risk it,
'cause I hadn't read all the way to the end
and if Harry was any sort of a friend
he wouldn't just leave me to hang there suspended
not knowing quite how the letter was ended,
and sputtering crumbs,
and wiping them off his shirt with his thumbs,
he started to read
exactly what was laid down in the screed
and I listened and blushed,
slowed him down when he rushed,
and wondered just what 'My Darling Kitten',
the person to whom the letter was written,
would make of the things that Harry reported
and whether she'd ever so gamely disported
and I pondered on how 'Sincerely your chum,'
the fellow from whom the missive had come,
had managed to make such detailed notes
whilst keeping a weather eye open for boats
and pedalo people out on the pond
(not folk, it was clear, of whom he was fond)
and at the same time still play a part
in breaking every heart

AF Harrold

he could find
including, to be honest, a portion of mine
and at the end of it all
Harry and I sat down in the hall
and cuddled a little
and calmly I wiped his chin clean of spittle,
the excitement was over, the kettle was whistling,
the hair on my cheek and my chin was now bristling
so I had a quick shave and a wash and a shower
and in just a little under an hour
I sat down in the study
with Harry, my buddy,
and we wrote a letter
(he spoke it out first then I typed it much better)
which we sent to the paper that's published each day
and it said in a tone sincere but gay
if you were expecting to learn about this
and that and some other all signed with kiss
and how he did what to whom and where
and when and how long all told with flair
and of course not forgetting this, this and that
then pull on your coat and put on your hat
for we have received your post by mistake
and we'll keep it safe if you bring the cake
and take tea with us,
the number 4 bus
stops just outside,
and after we've spoken for a bit we'll decide
just whether we'll let you go with your letter
or make you stay longer till we know you much better.

Liz Haywood

Liz has been scribbling all her life; she is interested in universal that can be found in the ordinary and Blakian ideas of 'joy and woe'. She works in Milton Keynes as a health visitor and lives in Bedfordshire in her newly-empty nest with her husband – more 'joy and woe' there then.

Liz Haywood

FOOTBALL FANS, THE DARK ARTS AND A MOTHER

It's all a bit kicky and shouty for me,
but you can't avoid it when
you live with three West Ham fans.
If only it was that simple,
and fortune was always hiding,
then they'd know where they were,
and could settle and make themselves
comfortable, somewhere in
the middle of the first (division).

But it plays fast and loose
And they're in and out,
up and down
The Premiership and Leagues
like the proverbial
fiddler's elbow and bride's nightdress,

Barometer, talisman
for all sorts of stuff –
so when The Hammers start winning
we get a new car
or one of the girls comes top in maths,
and it gets confusing,
and interconnected
and they really believe that one thing
can influence another in this way.

At the end of the day
I've turned Voodoo Lady,
albeit subconsciously;
last week, whilst toasting them for tea,
I burnt the Chelsea buns.

Liz Haywood

READER, I MARRIED HIM

And I can't tell you how awful it was.
What a miserable old git he turned
out to be. Miserable and mawkish,
addicted to being a victim, blind,
barely mobile and totally lost without
that bloody dog Pilot which lost it's
faculties shortly after my return,
slobbering all over my favourite silks,
and farting all day in the morning room.

My predicament makes me wonder what
became of dear Elizabeth Bennet
after her marriage to that prig Darcy.
Pretty much the same I imagine.
Endless evenings in listening to pompous
rants and of course the siring of the line.

And what about that little girl without
a name who married the marvellous Max
de Winter. We know it didn't start well
for them, but the rosy glow that morning,
the fire that was Manderley should have been
the dawn they mistook it for. Foolish
girl! I bet he proved as gloomy
with her as he had been with Rebecca.

What is it with us romantic heroines
That makes us think that beneath the storm clouds
We will find hidden depths of tenderness?

Liz Haywood

CONVALESCENCE

For forty-eight hours following surgery
I was every sick heroine
I have ever read about or seen.
Propped up on pillows,
two chairs at my bedside,
my room prepared as never before,
not even for those other great bedroom
scenarios – consummation and confinement.
I was Ali McGraw in *Love Story*,
tenacious in the face of fading hope,
Clara, Heidi's plucky foil and Cathy
dying unrequited. Supported by
my cast, my elder daughter
the only one to share the intimacy afforded
by sitting on my bed, her slender frame
barely denting the duvet, and making
no impact on my physical tenderness.
Sister, niece, parents and partner in a pinny
were followed by flowery friends.
The sips of soup, crumbs of cake
and sick room secrets were all delicious.
On the third day I rose again
and went to Sainsbury's

Liz Haywood

WORK IN PROGRESS

I am thousands of pounds short of the price
of a beach hut in Norfolk, but from April
to October I drink tea on porch steps.
And in winter keep a bowl of golden
gourds in my kitchen for their stored sunshine.

The words that should grow and mend my children
are often over seasoned, but our shared
lightening smiles for Mr Bean and Granddad
prove the pudding.

There are eighty three emails read but
undeleted in my inbox but by Friday
evening my desk is no longer
a Bank Holiday beach.

The hard skin on my feet is not the
greatest of my lover's worries,
but there are still soft places
for arrows to fall.

And yesterday, in a gallery
I saw a painting far more interesting,
beautiful even
than it would have been complete.

Liz Haywood

THE IMAGE OF HER

You look as if you have seen a ghost.
Shock imprints a face, heavy boots on wet mud,
I try to find some words
It happens to me sometimes when I look in the mirror.
It's her standing there -
with her direct blue eyes looking into mine.

With her direct blue eyes looking into mine,
It's her standing there.
It happens to me sometimes when I look in the mirror.
I try to find some words;
Shock imprints a face, heavy boots on wet mud.
You look as if you have seen a ghost.

BEING ENCOURAGED TO PARTICIPATE IN YOUR PARENT'S HOBBY

Tuesday night,practice night
climbing the spiral staircase
and three quarters up
the musty stench of the belfry
of dust trapped in fibres,
of carpets and sallies
of old men sweating into nylon.

Tuesday night, practice night
that sweet fusty smell
born from years and years
of those odd blokes who all
laughed at my jokes,ringing bells
for Sunday service and the hell of it

John Hegley

Mr Hegley was born in Newington Green, North London, and was educated in Luton, Bristol and Bradford University.

His first public performance monies came from busking his songs, initially outside a shoe shop in Hull, in the late Seventies. He performed on the streets of London in the early Eighties, fronting the Popticians, with whom he also recorded two sessions for John Peel, and has since been a frequent performer of his words, sung and spoken, on both local and national radio.

He has produced ten books of verse and prose pieces, two CDs and one mug, but his largest source of income is from stages on his native island. An Edinburgh Festival regular, he is noted for his exploration of such diverse topics as dog hair, potatoes, handkerchiefs and the misery of human existence.

John Hegley

I DIDN'T THINK THEY CALLED IT CONSTITUTION HILL FOR NOTHING

I spent a term in Birmingham
I went and caught a chill
I thought, now I'll let Birmingham
Illuminate this ill
I took no Beecham's powder
no reaching for the pill -
No linctus for my sphincters
no resort to the conventional,
my calumny to kill
I just took a constitutional
up Constitution Hill

*This arose when performing at the Birmingham Rep Theatre in "The Pyjama Game"
in 1999 and feeling under the weather.*

John Hegley

ANTS

An artist from Hartwell, Northants
entertained with his pictures of ants
He would draw them in houses
and six-legged trousers
but his spiders and earwigs
    were pants

*This one was devised as a publicity tool when performing at the Castle,
Wellingborough.*

TOM'S ECONOMY MEASURE

He would give you a mouthful would Tom
If you wanted your heating turning on
He would don one more sweater
And say, "That is better
Much better than metamorphosing a cartload of carbon emitting muck into
Yet another debilitating utility bill, John `

John Hegley

TRYING NOT TO DRIVE POEM

A merry car
is a car kept
slept
when walking
or wheel chairing
is a reasonable option:
The adoption of a greener alternative.
Set foot loose,
if you can
if you fancy.
Lace up
pace up
try to clean the pace up.
Can I have a lift?

*The above was composed originally for the website "Do the Green Thing"
as was the one about Tom and the pullovers.*

All the best
to you and the rest
of those who regularly speak
and the guests, at *Tongue in Chic*

John

Stephen Hobbs

Born into a military family (Grandfather, Father, Uncle and Cousin) Stephen (aka The Civilian) became a librarian; seeing action in Liverpool, Birkenhead, Bebington, Milton Keynes, and Bletchley. Raised on free school milk, English Timelords, and lots of fresh air; Stephen now sells books on CMK Market ("3 Trollopes a fiver") and believes that writing poetry is a serious and profound business – he really does. Now a grandfather himself, Stephen intends to make something of his life, and perhaps do something sensible.

Hobbscrazybooks@aol.com

ps: To Elizabeth

Stephen Hobbs

GREEN POEM

Of course, I walk to work –
one does one's bit.
I journey through the showers of Spring
the stair-rods of Summer,
Autumn's aquaness and Winter's watery wetness –
each season a reason for a lighter footprint.
And something profound strikes me as I roam –
I really must get a job closer to home

DOUBLE TALK

Bora Bora, Baden Baden, Ylang Ylang,
Talk Talk, Sing Sing, Duran Duran!
New York, New York – so good they named it twice.
Beri-Beri: not quite so nice.

Paw Paw, aye-aye, juju
JubJub, chi chi, frou frou
Dorothy Cotton of Eastenders fame
Dotco, dotco her website name.

TinTin, peri peri, TomTom,
tuk tuk, Pongo Pongo, bonbon:
Knock, County Mayo – for religious folk
Missed opportunity for a wonderful joke!

Stephen Hobbs

VASECTOMY

Right, she said, it's your turn now –
"family planning" don't make me laugh!
Osmosis, thrombosis, and a wire up me see you next Tuesday
that's 25 years of misery
you selfish bastard!
I took the hint, the phone numbers,
and the "You've only one child -
I don't think we can help
You'll have to go private".
That's pretty much what I was hoping for, I said
On a table in some god-forsaken shopping mall
Was not on my 1001 things to do before I die!

But private don't come cheap
and "special offers", "buy one get one free"
– don't make me laugh.
"You keep your socks on" the only concession I could get.
It's a hundred and fifty, you won't find cheaper
We've got it all sewn up!

So trousers round my ankles and socks pulled up
with just a little prick – leave it –
to numb me to the exquisite proximity
of stainless steel and testicles.
Smooooooth as a baby's bum –
you catch my drift –
DIY – no fun in that
and the aftershave a big mistake.

Stephen Hobbs

Very business-like the doctor and the nurse:
" I see the Dons are doing well" "Bin on yer olidays"
Pictures of children on the walls.
And then.....it was over!
I never heard the fateful snip
or the "Close up Nurse – I'm off to the opera!"
Just flush out the tubes – six weeks should do it.
Get your wife to help.
There may be some slight swelling
- you remember Spacehoppers?

In six weeks wank into this –
not quite his words – and we'll confirm your negativity.
It'll make a vas deferens to your life.
It's one we're obliged to make –
like crying over spilt milk.

So there you have it.
You can hardly see the scar.
And I have the written confirmation
to consider myself infertile.

Any regrets?
Well..... just the nagging thought
that if there were to be some world catastrophe
and I alone of all the males survived
and the repopulation of Planet Earth was down to me:
do I tell those females the truth –
or say nothing and just give it a go?

Stephen Hobbs

A PERFECT DAY

One day at school it all fell into place:
the corners, the straight bits –
you could read it plain as day.

Physics was never going to be fun,
Geography ruined what there was of it.
History was mostly about killing.

That meat was muscle,
that stamp collecting stopped,
when your testicles dropped.
That no-one said "racing cars", "jungle"
Or put "flippers" on their feet.

That girls couldn't catch for toffee,
but could fix you with a look to shame a shark.

That the secret thing you discovered
under the bed clothes listening to Radio Caroline
was pretty much common knowledge.

That most paedophiles were called Sir!

That it didn't matter if Dennis Kilby
was the handsomest boy in the class,
because his father had gone off the rails
and his mother liked a drink.

In short, all the stuff that makes the world tick.
And it was on that day that I was off sick!

Stephen Hobbs

REMEMBRANCE

A talking horse called Mr Ed
Kennedy's exploding head.

Biafran babies, screaming jets
"I want never gets".

Scratchy jumpers from your Nan
burning monks in Vietnam.

Bloody streets on black & white TV's
grammar and apostrophes

Slobodan Milosovicz
a dog that can say "sausages"

Forties, Cromarty, Fastnet
Helmand, Wootten Bassett

Frank Ifield in '62
"I remember you"*

The first single I bought! 7 weeks at number 1! Had a sell-out tour of the UK in '63 with The Beatles as his support band.

MY NEXT POEM

My next poem will astound!
"We had no idea"! they'll say,
Scintilla, shard, *and* cetacean.
I'll be between boards – not a staple in sight:
Reassuringly, prize-winningly slim -
that double f on the cover.
Serious reviews – "zeitgeist"
And "kaleidoscope of meaning".
They will read me in Swahili
I will be done in the curriculum
"A rare lapse into rhyme" – *The Guardian*.
Yes – just you wait for my next poem.

Richard Tyrone Jones

Richard Tyrone Jones is the Director of 'Utter!' spoken word (www.utterspokenword.com), one of the UK's best spoken word organisers, putting on shows at the Cross Kings, Whitechapel Art Gallery an Edinburgh festival. His first book, 'Germline', described by Edinburgh comedy award-winner Tim Key as 'Often witty, sometimes unsettling and always smart... bubbles with a nervy assurance and a frenetic energy' is selling very well. He has done over 400 gigs, is currently working on two new collections, a one-person show, more 'Utter!' events and (Mis)Guided tours, does educational workshops and should really get around to that novel...

Richard Tyrone Jones

A WARM WELCOME

Hello? Sorry, can I help you? Oh,
You're from where? Oh yes, of course,
We just heard about it on the telly.
Terrible Business.
Of course, one ought to make a gesture of solidarity, well,
Erm...come in, come in!
Would you like a cup of tea?

How many? Oh dear, yes, I lost a
brother last year. Go-karting. Tragic. Listen,
You seem a nice enough chap, if
You've nowhere to stay you can kip
In our lounge. For a bit. We've got a Futon.

Well, that probably won't be possible, see
Your region – sorry, country – has no oil or gas
And precious few emotional resources.
They won't help you claim it back.
Sorry if that's disheartening.
Would you like a cup of tea?

Look old chap, I've been meaning to broach this for the last few days;
We enjoy having you here, you're a very friendly man,
But it would be nice if you could somehow pay your way.
A few jobs need doing; there's the dusting, polishing –
You're a qualified engineer? Excellent! There are these shelves...

I mean we could convert the loft. If you help us do the job
You could stay up there. Or we don't really use the garage. I think it's all going
rather well so far. Your English is...
better and in a while we might be in a position to manage
To offer you a position at the shop – part time.
Who knows, One of your sons might even end up marrying our daughter –

not that one, the ugly one. Would you like a cup of tea?

Richard Tyrone Jones

SIMILE

Their fingers were like talons tearing at dead flesh
They pecked like vultures right down to the bones
Black scraps from their clothes flew like feathers in the air
When their sudden shrieks exploded like the caws of crows

That's because they were eating cold chicken at a fancy dress party both dressed
as birds and someone had just burst a balloon right next to them causing alarm.

< LIMITS OF LANGUAGE

This is not a treasure-trove of words, this is
Junk-shop language to describe a treasure-trove.
                       Watch these ones race like lemmings to the page's edge.
                              gimmick. a on hitching backtrack, these And

Here are my spells. This one is for a fire involving plastics.
Not on electrical goods now, apprentice!
And this incantation should anger a Muslim:
"Fuck Off Allah's gay pork is tasty yum yum."
Knock the door, clear the throat, recite and retire.

When is a door not a door? When it's a symbol.
Sit behind it and read till you've served out your sentence.
A pun's that wrong turning you took past the liminal,
For I sit and spin signs at the cross-roads of purpose.

Richard Tyrone Jones

ULTRA

The idea glowed as he was marking all his valuables,
'After all, I value you most', he joked, and so he dipped the nib
of his tongue in UV invisible ink,

intending to lick her all over, top to toe,
so he would know by any dark patch where he'd missed.
'But if you do that,' she laughed, 'and I do get lost

or stolen, they won't know where to return me! Leave room
for a postcode.' But he halted her tongue with his, proceeded to paint
her every surface. It didn't have to, but it took all night,

and some particularly hard-to-reach nooks were coated at least twice.
So when she stepped out naked onto the balcony of the flat
under the kitchen's blinking flycatcher and strip light

the denizens of the opposite blocks who swore they'd seen a ghost
were wrong; those who guessed a spirit were warmer;
those who said an angel: well, they only saw what I saw.

Theresa Kelleher

Theresa Kelleher is a performance poet and singer. Writing for just over two years, her varied styles are capturing audiences wherever she performs. Her dark and brooding poem "Bluebeard's On The Prowl Again" won her a place in the Finals of The Daffodil Theatre Awards 2009.

She has been invited to perform at The Stony Words Literature Festival 2010 where she will combine poetry, humour, drama and song. Her debut poem "There's a Fire in The Kebab Shop" a poem about community life, continues to delight new audiences. Writing about life, nature (both human and otherwise) the last year has seen several of her works published.

Theresa Kelleher

PORKIES AND DOORKEYS

Gorbals Mick, the first to speak and go in 300 years, shedding tears over fears in his beers with Hazel Blears.

What a way to handle, such a scandal, over MP's expenses, what defences, such pretences!

Ducks in huts, beds in sheds, soaps in moats, lawns and porn, patio heater, a pack of dorritas?

Taps and basins, skilled stone masons, kitchens fitted, jumpers knitted, tennis court repairs, office under stairs, a trouser press, designer dress, dinner to impress.....**"under duress"**.

Loos, views, lamps, ramps, mortgage expenses, repair of fences, under floor heating, No Sense of Cheating.

Pots and pans, hocks of ham, jams, clams, **SCAMS!**
Microwave oven? No Way to Govern.....

Grace and favour? Who can save her?
A house in Kent and then Brent East, two in Scotland, that's not the least, five in Deal and three in Cove, a flat in Keele and Brighton and Hove.

Sisters, Brothers, Lovers, Daughters too,
All of them enjoying perks paid for by me and you.

Honourable gentlemen now tumble, leaders lip fumble, parties will crumble, may become humble................Nah!

Dancing Vince Cable, born in a stable, becomes a fable, more motions to table.....

In our lifetime we have not seen the like!

Theresa Kelleher

But they are not to blame, it's the game, goes with the fame. It was the rules, they weren't acting like fools, reaping the jewels, behaving like mules.

They've done it for our good, to improve our neighbourhood. They've known for years it would end in tears, and aren't they great, though a bit too late, things are all going to.....drift.....start to.....shift!

Get More Scrutiny To Avoid A Mutiny

And now they're redacting, feels like retracting, make things more exacting, more mutual contracting.

It requires great leaps to gain trust from us peeps
So come on reform, to return to some norm.....

Critical Disinterest!

Theresa Kelleher

THE LIME

I once stood tall as a strong proud Lime,
But over the past two weeks of time,
A treeman took his axe to me
And now I'm a sprout of Broccoli.

Danni Kushner

A key player in the burgeoning Milton Keynes poetry/ performance scene, Danni, along with Fay Roberts, has taken the reins of the local poetry slam and re-branded it as Poetry Kapow!, (Milton Keynes' poetry/art/whatever performance events) since 2007. In 2009, Danni has been part of the roving crew of Milton Keynes poets, appearing at the Bedford and Coventry literary festivals, as well as becoming a regular fixture of poetry events in Northampton, Leamington Spa, and Leicester. She has performed extended sets at London's "Bang Said the Gun", Northampton's Umbrella Fair, and at the Edinburgh fringe. Danni's work always draws from personal experience, utilising intricate rhyme and meter, and she looks forward to an exciting 2010, beginning with a supporting slot at *Tongue in Chic*.

Danni Kushner

EDINBURGH

Metrolyptic
Warp, weft and cryptic,
These knotted streets, Painted, scripted.
Look up:
This crumpled mountain, embraced by ocean.
Awash with the splashed emotion
Of those thrusting themselves into this attrition,
Battling the elements and competition.
Look up:
This imposing fortress
Stacked bombastic monument of grandeur.
Noisily announcing itself with daily candour,
As this washing line of paper flowers,
Between these two towers,
Is the brightest-burning, attention-turning, affection-yearning
Spectacular explosion
Of stretched nerves, financial erosion.
Look up:
There is nothing that cannot be said,
Nothing that must not be seen.
If you have the will,
And the not inconsiderable means.
Be enchanted, enraptured,
Teased, tickled and captured.
Get lost, and then found,
And when you think you have mastered your path
On this hallowed ground
Look up.

Danni Kushner

AWEN

Warm waves of wide embraces
Misfits and outsiders with expectant faces.
The tracks of our years the bard traces,
And binds us all
With myth and lore.
For performance, respectful silence,
Between chatter and clatter and banter in canter.

The palm is compelled to the drum
Not shy of this ecstatic pulsation.
And in raising our spirits on this breaking surf
We ride – clung to this raft of our inspiration.

The gathering of this loyal few,
To share words of joy and the fruits of creation.
Each to their own selves are true,
Beneath the frivolity of this celebration.

The nights round these candles are warm
With tales and songs of invocation.
It's over too soon, so raise a glass to the moon
And to the spirit of our inspiration.

Danni Kushner

BLESS THIS...

This empty shell of memories that sheltered our growing pains
Needed scraping clean of history's remains.
So we're digging through belongings,
Mining for moments passed.
Through fashion's faded passions and hobbies that didn't last.
Through old hats, old shoes, old news,
Old 45s of jives and Blues,
Old games, old picture frames,
Faded photos of old flames.
School reports, so well hid.
"Must try harder" Never did.
Scalextrix, Hornby, Spirographs,
Cluedo, Ludo chess and draughts.
Mix tapes, aged videos and in-between
Rolls of cine-film and a crooked screen.

The dusty projector rick-a-ticks
Like a card in the spokes of my old BMX
Stars of silent films we are
With previous pets, and mum's first car.
In canal holiday heat-waves and Christmas snow up to our knees,
In fields where now just houses stand,
With the ghosts of last year's trees.

Amongst the hat boxes and sepia photographs
We reminisce, share tears and laughs.
And when you wonder why you kept these things remember:
Though it now stings, feel the joy this remembrance brings.
These artefacts won't change our pasts,
Or affect our future paths,
But for just this moment of rediscovery
These ingredients spark an alchemy that allows us to let go.
Yet every night since then,
In my convoluted dreams
This house is always home.

Danni Kushner

CONCRETE

Living in the city, feeling un-pretty,
Growing slowly dizzy over the nitty-gritty.
When the air is full of poison and the night is never still,
Handing out promises never to fulfil.
And it doesn't like your face when you cannot stand the pace.
You're looking for a bridge to jump
Over the rat-race.
Sanity is relative under these demands
Don't dare to crack up you won't get a second chance
Making last-ditch phonecalls to hear a level voice
"Can't speak to you right now, better make another choice"
You're looking for an exit in the shadows of your life,
With the train tracks calling you to cut you like a knife.
Don't know why you cannot handle it,
Looking at your friends,
Seeing how they're doing fine,
Burning at both ends.
But you underestimated
This life so over-rated.
Emaciated with your hopes so soon degraded.
In the place that you call home tonight
You let the clouds descend,
Let the voices slowly shatter
As you begin to mend.
Try not to think of morning when you'll hear them all again.
And in the sanctity of solitude
You sleep in some distress,
Dreaming of train-tracks
And emptiness.

Craig Lambert

Craig Lambert

SON DAYS

I heard the rasp of the saw.
Like the breathing of a dying man,
harsh, splintered. Moving
through your strong hand.
'Thank you' nods accepted wood, felt
and nails. They bound us to that time.
Our conversations short through the moving
of years dropped from this child's small hand.
When adolescent grown I often felt
the bindings loosen. Yet still I saw
in you, the strength of love that makes a man.
'Thank you' nods would do until we found the time.
I heard the breathing of a dying man,
like the rasp of a rusted saw.
Harsh, splintered. Moving.
I held your frail hand.
'Thank you' I heard you say and felt
acceptance bind us through the end of time.

For my dad, Derek Lambert 1929-2007

Craig Lambert

THE SPIDER AND THE FLY

You walk soft mouthed, move unknown ways
speaking waft webbed, sounding the spider
who I the insect, cannot comprehend.
Captured as the victim of our fate.
This room had been ours while we evolved the
leisure light of heat-wave love-days swarm,
to the worry buzz of flies laying eggs,
and now; grey cobweb words hang in my ears.
Helpless to your strangling honesty
the thread you spin around my neck so tight,
squeezes the juice of my digested life
'til heart, head burst, collapse and fall away.
The cell of every fibre of my trust
crushed by four words showing your eight legs.
I only want six so this is my death.
We have grown together, changed together,
but neither is the same as evolution.

Craig Lambert

STARGAZER

Eventually the sun rolled over the horizon.
I watched the glaze of its orange echo
fade to autumn gold, like other winter days.
My toes gripped the sand as if holding a memory
of when this island was our place of poetry, music
the soft sun-swept swimming haze of dreams
sung in telepathic tune, unhindered by the clock.

I found my fingers snaking upwards for your hand
but as the final breath of twilight slipped by
the moon fell on my shoulder like a frozen rock,
silvering the cooler air to reveal a shadow face
that saw me, knew me, drew me three years older
to beyond the hugs and kisses of your voice.
Further still, still further, the wondrous stars.

I looked up at the night to see which one is you
hoping to see you there, but wanting you here
beside me, gazing at the stars as one bright us.
This I miss and much more that is beautiful,
tender, sensual and strong in all I crave of you.
To kiss your lips and taste immortal song
in the universal galaxy of our consciousness.

Yet, here within the silent beating of my heart
and in treasures that you buried in my mind,
I sense you moving, feel you dancing, free.
I still cry but my heart does not need to mourn.
My joy is in wanting you to fly. For that is love.
No longer beside me, but deep inside me
and still as new and hopeful as the dawn.

Craig Lambert

COMMUNION

Mr Davies arrives at the Cathedral.
Taking his seat with a satisfying
sense of ownership, he nods and smiles
at colleagues and acquaintances.
Such long suffering souls bound in fellowship
have witnessed the seasons as one,
never knowing which days are Spring,
Summer, Autumn or Winter until they have gone.
That is the magic of this place. An elusive
dream hovers above imagination,
occasionally drawn in by the breath of hope.
Then exhaling nervous energy, willing God's
intervention, false prophets vent their rage.
Frustration takes its toll, passion washes sorrow
in acoustic harmony. Mr Davies is alive
to the frenzy, licked by the lustre of tomorrow.
This is his Church, his home, his spiritual heart.
A lifetime of faith instilled by his father
who first brought him here, in wide eyed magnitude?
forty years ago, to witness the prayers of atheism
and believe that one day they will be proven wrong.
As the congregation sway and sing, he sings too,
but silently within. A shy man who lives alone
except here, where barely noticed he feels new.
Each fortnight his sad life is invested completely
on grounds of worship, in mourning heroic ghosts.
He never lets them down and never will.
Then, suddenly Saturday becomes Summer.
The rain beating down on tin roofs applauds
and resonates joy, the rattling seats an energy spill
of orgasmic exaltation. Strangers leap and hug.
Mr Davies briefly finds God again. One nil.

Craig Lambert

LESS, IS MORE OR LESS MORE.

Pestilence avails itself of the crops.
The sun scoops a share to the convex
bowl of its generous convection,
copper coating a crust to the earth
at which men hack with sticks. Their
corrugated cattle drag tired tongues over
dregs of stagnant pools, oblivious to thin
lipped clouds stealing sips through the straw.
Seeing seedlings wither on the harrowing dust
and the skeletons of vegetation collapse,
children learn to aspire to subsistence;
to engage in Nature's civil war, the imploding
tribes of feast and famine and the elegant
impasse between element and sacrament.
If a hungry man surveys his parched plot
he may wonder where he stands
in the food chain.................................Or why.
Yet later, huddled in the shade of shacks,
orchestrating the orbit of a communal bowl
to the gentle rhythm of simple utensils,
a family can find itself at the apex of creation.

David Lovesy

David Lovesy is a riddle, wrapped in a mystery, inside an enigma, covered in batter and lightly fried with a delightfully cheesy topping.

David's life completely revolves around comedy. Even his day job is a farce. He regularly performs with his comedy improvisation group "Whose Turn?" to sell-out audiences, and if that wasn't challenge enough he also contracted a curious condition known as "fatherhood". The sleepless nights, the time spent elbow deep in muck and the constant tantrums: still, that's amateur dramatics for you. Small children are probably easier to deal with.

Having lived in Milton Keynes all his life, David has already proven what a sense of humour he must have. Part of a three man writing team (TLC Creative) he has authored many pantomime and playscripts which are performed internationally (recently selling performance rights of 2001 Arabian Nights to Dubai: still not sure if they thought it was a documentary).

David Lovesy

NEED

I need you like a pop song needs a bridge
Like Ultravox needs Midge
Which means nothing to me
Oh! Vienna.

I need you like a cornet needs a flake
Like an arctic roll needs cake
Which means much more to me
Oh! Viennetta.

What am I saying?
Am I puncturing the dream
When I say I don't like Ultravox
But like to eat ice cream?

Yes, probably. I'm shallow like that.

David Lovesy

HAPPENSTANCE

I've started a diet to drop a few pounds
I was told it was needed on medical grounds
So it's protein for lunch, green salad at night
The concept is fine but the food's just not right
So a lifestyle of swimming and long urban walks
And evenings just munching on celery stalks.

My pet pussy Tiddles is feeling the strain
His poor nether regions are in quite some pain
Just under his tail is a swollen red boil
That is soothed with a gentle massaging of oil
Sweet little moggy, asleep in the sun
Slowly appeased from the cyst on his bum.

I'm also rehearsing to be in a show
A staging of eighties hit 'Allo 'Allo
With my physique I can only play Colonel von Strohm
Which my natural skills help me do with aplomb
But the costume has braces with clasps that don't work
So the trousers fall down if I stand with a jerk.

So when you walked in and caught me off guard
Whilst dressed as a Nazi, smearing Tiddles with lard
A handful of celery being given a squeeze
And my trousers dropped shabbily down by my knees
You thought you had trespassed on an aberration
But I TOLD you that there was a good explanation.

Paul Lyalls

Paul Lyalls' work is funny, fast-moving, hip, accessible, rhythmic, clever and real. He has run hundreds of workshops in secondary and primary schools, youth projects and prisons. As a performance poet, Paul has gigged 10 Edinburgh Festivals and many prestigious venues in cities as diverse as New York to Belfast. In 2008 Paul was Poet for the London Borough of Brent, becoming the first poet to perform at the New Wembley stadium. Paul presented and starred alongside former World Poetry Slam Champion Kat Francois in the BBC/CBBC television programme 'The Big Slam Poetry House'.

Paul Lyalls

THE VALUE OF WALES

Its chief contribution to the UK
must be as a unit of measurement,
As night after night
a news desk declares
'An area of Rainforest,
the size of Wales disappears every year'
'The amount of water
London loses through its creaking Victorian pipes
would fill a swimming pool
the size of Wales'.
Every part of the world has a similar unit of measurement:
in the United States it's an area the size of New Jersey;
on mainland Europe the reference more often than not
is Slovenia – which appropriately happens to be
98.4 percent *the size of Wales*.
But just how accurate is Wales
as a unit of measurement?
Just how constant is that land-mass?
It's worth remembering that at low tide
Wales measures 20,761 SQ KM.
Whereas at high tide, it's only 20,449 SQ KM
and to really put it into context,
each year coastal erosion erodes an area of Wales
the size of Central Swansea.
For those of you in Europe trying to visualise this,
that's the equivalent of an area the size of down-town Ljubianna.

Paul Lyalls

TIME

Our hotelier pointed out that
all the clocks in all the hotel rooms
all said different times.
So, in some rooms you were late
and in other rooms you were early.
"It's not a problem", said the Nuclear Physicist
breakfasting on the next table
"Time actually happens four times slower than
we think"?
"Not round here it doesn't!" rejoined our hotelier,
"Round here, time happens really fast."
At which, I gazed out of the window
and surveyed the lifeless two street
regional-coastal town –
which had about as much going
on as a letter that never arrives.
If ever there was an
argument for there not being a God,
this place was it.
"In fact," continued our hotelier, "you can tell
how much is going on around here
by the all the things that are happening:
in September there's a Wicker Doll fair,
in October a Poetry Festival and a Science Convention,
in November there's Bonfire Night
and before you know it,
it's Christmas.
Right, who's got time for another cup of tea?"

Paul Lyalls

THE ANATOMY OF A BOOKSHOP

English Literature
was beside the drinking fountain.
American literature
was over near the vending machine.
Romance,
next to the fire escape.
Philosophy
was between the first and second floors.
Crime
could be found next to the tills.
Politics
was below ethics.
Self-help,
by the mirror.
Making The World A Better Place
was next to books on children's names.
Religion
was next to Fantasy.
Poetry,
Was down in the basement
with Wines, Beers and Spirits.

Paul Lyalls

HARD FAST AND BEAUTIFUL

In John Ford's Stagecoach (1939),
(which raised the Western genre
to artistic status)
she was the 'saloon girl' Dallas
who had been forced out of town
by puritanical women.
When 'The Ringo Kid' (John Wayne)
proposes to her, she says
"But you don't know me,
you don't know who I am."
"I know all I want to know."
he says.
Seeing a glimmer of hope
she asks the drunken doctor
(Thomas Mitchell)
"Is that wrong for a girl like me?
If a man and a woman
love each other?
it's all right,
ain't it Doc?"

Isobelle Madden

Isobelle Madden

HOSPICE DAYS

Sometimes the lake was still, a mirror to moonlight.
Sometimes the wind cut it into dark jagged edges.
Sometimes it filled and filled with the tears
of heavy clouds, hanging low.

Beyond the garden it pulled our gaze.
And even with blinds drawn we fed it our mood -
a grass lined flood of the changing
shapes, colours and smells of our days.

Inside the hospice we watched the door sign dance
to where death stopped. Waiting as it jumped
the corridor – turning up stealthy after tea
and asking us to see the nurse in charge.

And when it finally settled with us we were rarified –
exotic in our mystery to those still waiting.
Half believing the dance would not find them
half hoping it would find them soon.

Sometimes the lake is still, a mirror to moonlight.
Sometimes the wind cuts it into dark jagged edges.
Sometimes it fills and fills with the tears
of heavy clouds, hanging low.

Isobelle Madden

REGRET

I heard her first —
a neonatal wail
refracted through my
rear view mirror.

Second glance
revealed a small doe.
Howling as the flesh was
ripped from her rump.

Watching the life blood ooze
from the obscene, shivering
mess of her thigh,
I froze with rage.

But the dog lunged again,
tugging at the wound
and I screeched
at his red wagging face.

With a sly swipe I
caught the collar
of a happy stray.
Messy with death.

We watched. She kicked
a ravaged, tattered torso
into the hedge row,
beyond the neatly kept park.

I should have let him
finish the job.

Isobelle Madden

GREAT GRAND MOTHER.

Head high to her mothers hip
she knew, like she knew how to breathe,
the curve of that buttock and the feel
of the strong, rigid thigh beneath
that chained her to life -
kept her upright
on a slimey organic floor.

If she looked upwards she
could see the flaccid underside of
her brother, held too tightly
to a dry breast.
Cradled too fast for breath.

She learned silence then and crept,
when she could, into that space
between maternal feet and belly.
Her brother's body for cover
and the smell of fear for air.

So when she was grasped
in rough white hands,
she remembered only terror
and her mothers released grief
as the stale water flushed down
her scabbed and swollen throat.

Isobelle Madden

RIP TIDE

Out of my reach
the blue and yellow ball bobs -
leads me further from shore.
I cannot grasp it
and beyond my depth
I turn, mourning the loss.

But my legs – spaghetti
in the current – won't push
hard enough. I shout,
dragging leaden arms through
heavy water.
I pull the sea from me,
but it blocks my
way to the beach.

I am unheard
in the screams of toddlers,
playing safe by parents.

I am unseen,
Fighting seaweed
And burning lungs.

Isobelle Madden

I am boneless.

     All spent.

          Done in.

               Alone.

I give my body
to the passage of the ball
and the sea turns me.
I marvel at my easy pace -
racing past rocks

          and out,

               and out,

                    and out.

I look up and
slam
into the chest of my father
wading towards me,
carrying a large
blue and yellow ball.

Mark Niel

Mark lives in Milton Keynes and has been active on the local arts scene for many years. This was mainly in the theatre where he wrote, acted and directed. Mark has written poetry throughout his life and occasionally shared them in public for special occasions such as Christenings. Encouraged by the publication of a couple of poems in Monkey Kettle, he ventured to take an Open Mic spot at Poetry Kapow in May, 2008. Although this was one of the scariest things he'd ever done, the warm and enthusiastic response he received kick-started his ambition to be a poet.

Since then, Mark has sought out opportunities to perform and was inspired by some of the wonderful events he attended. This led to the founding of Tongue in Chic. Mark quickly found his feet as a performance poet and won a number of Slams including the Camden Crawl, Hammer and Tongue, Farrago, and the Bilston Big Love Slam. He has also been published in a number of anthologies and magazines and won a written poetry competition.

Mark continues to enjoy writing and performing and you can keep up to date with his news and performances at his website "A Kick in the Arts".

www.akickinthearts.co.uk

Mark Niel

DAWN

You lied about your age,
Your weight and your shoe size.
I found out too late
To halt our demise.

Half truths and whoppers
Comprised your diction.
No facts, just fantasy
And falsehoods and fiction.

This dress? Just ten pounds,
Bought in a sale.
If your nose was Pinocchio's
It would run off the scale.

You deceived and destroyed me
At every wrong turn.
Took wallet and dignity
And left me, heartburned.

So I'm both broke and broken
At the first light of morn.
In more than one way,
You were another false Dawn

LOST

A chocolate ocean
Laps sponge cake shores.
From marshmallow clouds
Spiced sugar pours

Dusting marzipan trees,
And sticky toffee highlands
Yes, I'm macarooned
On a dessert island

Mark Niel

HALF LIFE DAY (9 July, 2008)

Dark, dark and dark the night
as we walked, squeezing the last moments
from the weekend before work
usurped our time.

Bright, bright and bright the stars
that pinpricked the velvet indigo
and eavesdropped our whispered
intimacies.

Soft, soft and soft your face
I held
as creeping certainty
came calling.

Sweet, sweet and sweet your kiss
as together falling
from casual romance
to soul certain permanence.
Impromptu proposal
met with a breathless "Yes".

Quick, quick and quick the years
once constant companion
now distant acquaintance
taking our moments
for souvenirs.

Mark Niel

Cold, cold and cold the days
when sorrow shared our souls.
Rain cloud shadow
a weeping canopy
blocking the sunlight.

Hard, hard and hard the words
at times as edge on edge
we smoothed and shaped
each other
fashioning a better fit.

Deep, deep and deep the love
that remains ingrained
making one from two.
So I stand on Half Life Day
the man I am,
because of you.

Mark Niel

AFAR

I. Want. You.

The light of you,
The night of you.
The power, the strength, the fight of you.

The nerve of you,
The verve of you.
Every sensuous curve of you.

The dawn of you,
The dusk of you.
The flesh, the shell, the husk of you.

The arts of you,
The smarts of you.
The hidden, delicious parts of you.

The heart of you,
The soul of you.
Nothing-but-the-truth whole of you.

The heat of you,
The beat of you.
The warm and wet and sweet of you.

The near of you,
The far of you.
The sun and moon and stars of you.

The sight of you,
The bite of you.
The quivering delight of you.

Please. Want. Me.

Mark Niel

HOW TO ANNOY PENGUINS (1)

If you ever see a couple of penguins,
And wish to annoy him or bate her,
Just click your fingers
and say quite sharply
"Waiter".
They'll hate ya!

HOW TO ANNOY PENGUINS (2)

Here's another way to annoy penguins
if you're prepared to risk it
Shout "Oi mate, I've seen you on the telly
Or was it on a biscuit?"

HOW TO ANNOY PENGUINS (3)

- Fuel global warming, causing temperatures to rise and their breeding grounds to melt.
- Ignore the fact the coldest environments feel the effects first and most severely.
- Reduce numbers of krill, the main source of food for some penguins.
- Take more fish out of the oceans than is sustainable, leading to the extinction of some species.
- Stand idly by, unhelping and unthinking while penguins stand (literally) on increasingly thin ice.

Sorry! We're already doing that.

Niall O'Sullivan

Niall O'Sullivan has released two collections of poetry, *you're not singing anymore* and *Ventriloquism for Monkeys*, with Flipped Eye. He has performed poetry all over the UK and Europe for over ten years. In 2009, Niall featured on BBC Radio and Television during his residency at the 2009 Wimbledon Tennis Championships. He runs London's biggest open mic poetry night, *Poetry Unplugged*, every Tuesday at the Poetry Café.

Niall O'Sullivan

POEM FOR ALL THE OLD MEN THAT STILL HAVE ELVIS HAIRCUTS

I saw one of them getting off the number 3
outside Brixton Town Hall this morning.
He must've been in the last five years of his working life,
but he still had a full head of hair
and he wasn't afraid to use it.
Same cut he must've had since way back
when his best mate pulled hot black vinyl
from a crisp white sleeve, snarling
you aint heard nothin' yet
with a newfound curl to his lip.
After that there came the hard blip
of the needle hitting the groove
and what happened next
was enough to send our boy home
to plunge his fingers into a tub of Brylcreem
and baptise himself
He kept on doing it
through strike and recession
through moon landings and flower power,
even as hair sprouted from his ears
and his abdomen echoed the Vegas years,
he kept on doing it because nothing else
had hit him so hard, searing his soul
and leaving him all shook up, *uh-huh-huh*.
Look out for them; they're everywhere
standing out from the other fickle generations
like a well-pronounced ring on an oak tree's trunk
signifying that in that particular year
conditions were suddenly extreme
and unpredictable.

Niall O'Sullivan

A ONCE-FAMOUS VENTRILOQUIST LEARNS TO COPE WITH THE DRUDGERY OF A NORMAL LIFE

He still scrapes the odd buck
from his most famous creation,
university shows with the odd F-word
to acknowledge his audience have matured.
Halfwit the Hippo and Lord Lovelunch
didn't kick up a storm on e-bay.
His new voices are slightly skewed
variations of the same theme:
a confident chirp for the bank manager,
a geezerish growl down the pub,
and of course, the stage voice
whenever he's recognised at B&Q.
He cleans a few windows to get by,
mostly for friends of friends
catches his weary reflection
as he swipes away the suds,
tries to think of it as another puppet
brilliantly operated by a subtle mind.
Come evening, he dozes
in front of the flicker of his old stage,
the ache of his muscles the symptom
of a new self he's building
like the meal ticket he once fashioned
in his father's cluttered shed.
Goodnight my love, he whispers
as he kills the bedside lamp.
Goodnight my darling, I'm so proud of you!
replies the photograph of his ex-wife
pronouncing the p in proud
with passion and precision.

Niall O'Sullivan

MY CITY

I guess it's somewhere between the twinkle
of Canary Wharf's tip and the last drip
from a sleeping tramp's trouser leg
to trickle down a Soho drain.
Lower still, to the electric trains
that whirr through the dark, the fickle
haircuts of Hoxton, the markets and their tacky crap,
the ghosts of rippers, working girls, the smog.
The river, of course, the river, it's up to you
whether you picture the sunlit glitter
of its surface, or maybe below
for sand, old bones, yesterday's litter.
Tonight's recommendation is my bed.
If not, bollocks, buy an A-Z.

Niall O'Sullivan

CRANES

after the wrecking ball
has swished through the mortar
made the old building
a churning pith of Victoriana
we call for the cranes
to wake and wheel
from their dark barns
all clunky and clenched
they shall rise
arch their necks
over the highest roofs
solemnly begin
slow work their weaving
bidding girders to stand
like fumbling giraffe calves
lifting blocks like newborns
five individuals
or one whole hand?
our city a puppet
beneath their long strings?
come evening they spool up
their hook tongues   face
each other in conference
grow permafrost beards
their work is soon done
a glass palace for the
yellowcaps to furnish
for their pinstripe kings
and then they shall wilt
surrender the skyline
retreat to their nests
of barbed wire and tin

Rachel Pantechnicon

Poet, 43, with a veritable cornucopia of verses, stories and observations. Specialises in motivational poems for cats and for people. Rachel is many things: the best-dressed woman on the poetry circuit; the woman who won the 2004 Glastonbury Festival Poetry Slam, although she only entered it for the experience (and was perhaps the only person on site wearing court-shoes); and the author of the well-known story-books about Cheesegrater Leg-Iron Lion. In short, a most peculiar talent.

Rachel Pantechnicon

FOUR MAGNOLIA WALLS

Four magnolia walls was all I wanted,
four magnolia walls was all I wanted.
Once you were a geography teacher,
now you are a decorator.
All I wanted was my four magnolia walls
and what I didn't want was what I got:
you painted me a mural of a diagram
of an aerial view of a bird's-foot delta –
alluvial deposits yellow, bright blue for the water,
the course of the river corresponding
to an existing hairline crack.
Geography teacher decorator, geography teacher decorator,
geography teacher decorator, don't come back.
All I wanted in my bathroom
was the normal style of tiling – white tiles, horizontal,
every seventeenth tile with a picture of a seashell.
What I didn't want was every seashell annotated
in Humbrol paint, approximately dated
to its nearest geological era,
telling me if it's a bivalve, a brachiopod or a lamellibranch.
Geography teacher decorator, geography teacher decorator,
geography teacher decorator, don't come back.
Underneath the ceiling, ornamental frieze:
stencilled lettering spelling out the principal industries
of the principal towns in Northamptonshire –
Wellingborough: boots & shoes
Kettering: boots & shoes too
Corby: steel
Brackley: wool
Daventry: unknown.
Geography teacher decorator, geography teacher decorator,
geography teacher decorator, actually that's quite useful –
could you do me something similar with Rutland
in the vestibule?

Rachel Pantechnicon

GREAT GOD QUETZALCOATL GREEN HOT-WATER BOTTLE COVER

No more eiderdowns for me,
no extra sheets or electric socks -
there's a new accoutrement in my blanket-box:
I've got a great god Quetzalcoatl green hot-water bottle cover -
a present from my aunt and uncle
from their trip to Central America –
Uncle Barry, Auntie Erica,
both explorers, that's how they met -
they both simultaneously discovered
the source of the River Ganges.
Half an hour either way, they'd've missed each other,
wouldn't have met.
Life's funny like that.
Anyway, they said 'Rachel, we've got you
a great god Quetzalcoatl green hot-water bottle cover.
We hope you like it -
it was either that or a pillowcase shaped like the god of spring
with a skull for a face and his liver on the outside,
but they didn't do them in lavender
and we know you like lavender.'
But I like my great god Quetzalcoatl green hot-water bottle cover:
one half's feathery, the other half's scaly,
because of the dual nature of the deity -
part bird, part snake, part snake, part bird.
The feathery half keeps me awake, tickles my middle,
makes me laugh;
the scaly half gives me nightmares about lizards
and in that respect it's a lot like life –
partly nice and partly nasty.

Rachel Pantechnicon

TEENYBOP THEOLOGIAN

When I was teenage – difficult age -
I was into the Protestant Reformers:
posters of Calvin and Zwingli on my wall,
autographed copy of the Papal Bull
("To Rachel, love Leo X, PS you're excommunicated").
My enthusiasm could never be sated:
on the phone to my friend Katie -
"Did you see him yesterday?
You know who – in the churchyard at Wittenberg -
isn't he dead gorgeous though?"
Oh
Saturday morning, meeting Katie
in the Wimpy or the Golden Egg -
tartan trousers halfway up our legs,
tartan armbands, tartan anklesocks,
tartan scarf saying "I Love John Knox" -
because this week in *Jackie* they did Presbyterians
(Questionnaire: How Presbyterian Are You?)
and now we're doing scrapbooks.
I said to Katie "I know who you fancy"
"Who?" she says
"That bloke out of the Lollards" I say
"No I do not, Rachel you old moo -
anyway, I believed in rejecting the doctrine of transubstantiation
before you."
Oh
Saturday night, youth-club disco,
can of Tizer in my hand growing warm -
boy comes up to me, looks at my t-shirt,
says "Hello, I see you're into Reform"
"Might be" I say
"Yes, me too – what do you think of the Edict of Worms?"
"It's all right" I say
"Yes, it's good, isn't it? What do you think of the Edict of Nantes?"
So I slapped him round the face -
next he'd be asking me if I wanted to dance.
But he was all right, though – really quite nice -
and he did look a little like Martin Luther -
but don't they all under the disco lights?

Rachel Pantechnicon

ELF-SHELF

Unsolicited pixies slipping through my letterbox again;
I put them on the elf-shelf, put them on the elf-shelf.
Hobgoblins in the HobNobs taunting me again;
I put them on the elf-shelf, put them on the elf-shelf.
Goblins gobbling up the teabags,
saying "Here's how tea's made, Rachel, go and stuff yourself."
I put them on the elf-shelf, put them on the elf-shelf.
Breakfast cereal on the table – there it is, Snap Crackle & Pop – making me feel
uncomfortable;
must be those gnome things on the box.
I put them on the elf-shelf, put them on the elf-shelf.
Ring at the doorbell: oh no, it's the shelving elf, the shelving elf – tinkling bell on
the end of his hat –
saying "Madam, I've come to inspect your elf-shelf:
rawl-plugs, brackets, things like that"
and he hangs up his little gossamer jacket
with the orange fluorescent stripe across the back
and says to me, "Two toadstool spores in my cup of tea please love...
oh dear dear dear" he says, "oh no no no" he says,
"I do not like the look of that –
that elf-shelf isn't hanging level –
look at that corner, should be nicely bevelled –
somebody could have their eye out."
I shout "Listen here, you little piskey"
and I scoop him up on the elf-shelf shovel
and shovel him onto the elf-shelf.
And now there's unsolicited pixies slipping through my letterbox again;
I put them on the elf-shelf, put them on the elf-shelf.
Latchkey leprechauns through the catflap,
lapping up the Senior Feline Science-Plan crunchies;
a never-ending battle, eh?
I wonder what the cat'll say.

Fay Roberts

Fay is a 35-year-old classically-trained singer from Cardiff who started performing at the age of 4. She has been getting stuff published since slightly later. She started writing poetry regularly after being encouraged by the fabulous Monkey Kettle magazine. She was bitten by the performance poetry bug in Spring 2006 after a favour to a friend turned into a place in the final of a poetry slam.

She co-manages a series of live poetry events (Poetry Kapow!) with the rather fabulous Danni Antagonist in Milton Keynes, performs in various parts of the Midlands and South East, and is part of a Milton Keynes poetry collective calling themselves Bardcore. She currently a professional pedant, still sings in choirs and everywhere else and, since summer 2009, is based in Cambridge.

Fay's work has been described as: "lyrical", "engaging", "scarily good" and, memorably: "there were too many words... I got lost..." Her voice has been described as "musical", "mellifluous", and "mesmerising".

Fay has performed poetry in Milton Keynes, Leicester, Coventry, London, Leamington Spa, Northampton, Bedford, and Stowe; in Open Mic, festivals, showcases, collaboration, competition and costume. Sometimes she bangs a drum and has appeared on the same bill as a whole bunch of scarily good people it feels like arrant name-dropping to mention, many of whom came about as a result of the awesomeness that is *Tongue in Chic's* Mark Niel...

Find out more at www.faithhope.co.uk
Poetry Kapow! is at www.poetrykapow.co.uk

Fay Roberts

TURNING POINT

And so the longest day of the year sped by
Lifted on the smiling backs of gulls
And tugged on by the breeze that graced us
There on our hill, watching the sky wheel overhead.

My flesh still warms to that sun's caress
on your skin.
My smile still remembers your hand –
Heavy with the softness of you.

There was a kite
And the crash of surf below us.
There were distant shouts,
And the brief, wet nose of a questing dog.
There were the scents of crushed grass
And your hair – spun glass on the breeze
Reaching out.

I'll swear we passed a lifetime there,
In that echoing day that rushed past us,
Taken on the tide of words spoken
And words silent.
And I'll swear at the last your dandelion breath
Puffed the summer stars into the sky
That hushed with the dying of the day.

The force that pricked them through it
Pushed me to my back
Where the earth gently gifted me the day's heat
And I, awed, wept for it all:
Two tiny tears I passed off as hayfever.

Fay Roberts

We left before the night grew cold.
And you believed me.

The bedrock of my soul
Still gives back the heat of that day
I only have to close my eyes
And I'm half-blinded again by midsummer sunlight,
Lost in the place of the new colours
Seen obliquely by the sun through your eyes.

I cannot remember one word of that day.
Not even your name.
And so its treasure is secure.
High on its everlasting hillside.

Fay Roberts

I HOPE I'M IN CLOVER

Some people are like plants
the gardener never intended.
And I mean that in a
whole host of ways.

Like the bright-tongued
dandelion people.
Putting down roots in other people's patches,
Networking on every breath of wind.

Bramble folk sprawl, broad-shouldered
Laughing sharply at attempts to move them
Shifting to block your way
At every turn.

Others lurk on the borders
Weak-looking and pale,
No barbs or stings, just a quiet rustling.
Yet every day... there are more of them.

I knew a woman once like rosebay willowherb;
Thriving on the sites of disasters
Softening shrapnel-sharp edges
With bold velvet splash.
Laugh like an incongruous purple boa
Among the widow weeds.

Fay Roberts

IN DARKNESS

If you're seeking guidance this month,
look up.
Venus lights the sky;
a wet and naked,
full-grown birth
set to music,
dancing to the waves' order.
A name to bind the cruel,
moist, hardening fire;
the dark, organic cleft beneath the
marble lines of Governance.

From this insistent voices issue,
prophesying ivy to twine
around those columns,
birds to nest in gap-toothed roofs,
and those stiff lines softened,
broken and concealed
by weather, theft and newer gods,
whose love is spoken differently.

As you travel, you will find that
Names can be slippery.
Up where the sea is colder,
and these waves crash heads and
foam at the lips, follow Loki's light –
a spear thrown across the sea
to bring ash and blood spurting
from a lust for gold and screams.

And further yet,
In another country,
that bright, consuming mystery
has yet another name.
For love of freedom,
Lucifer ignites the eastern sky.

Fay Roberts

THE BREATH OF THE SOUL

The breath of the soul is flawed,
Scored with the indentations that caressed,
That brought it here, that made it what it is.

The sigh that is stone rolls, as it must
Making tracks, as it goes, in the dust –
Black and white and, later, gold.

The essence of the stone is the groans heaved
in its weaving, the sweat poured,
The flesh and blood beaten against its surface,
The heart worn with each sharp stroke
shaping the whole, bestowing grace,
carving a face into this change of nature.

And when the last stroke is taken,
The stone rolls to the centre of the room
where all turns on its axis for a while;
a sweet and bitter while.
Until time passes and dust falls,
Changing its shape again, softening its shadow.

For perfection is in the making
and when the breath stops...
the sigh is still.
And all that is left of the stone
are the tracks that it made as it passed through
the dust of the world
Which keeps on turning.

(for James Lee Byars and Alex Smith)

Guy Russell

Guy Russell

A PAPER AEROPLANE

Hey, love gods of the air-conditioned air
She's that one, in the third row of benchettes
That perfect neck beneath the perfect hair
And earlobes which have launched a thousand jets.

Gods, bless my shy and slightly wobbly take-off
Guide me across the headtops, down the rows
Below the radar of the busy prof
And well away from Andrew Ebbs, who knows,

Then near that thin gold chain above her jumper
Turn me for the approach. In a smooth glide
Touch me down safely on her pad, and bump her
With my keen nose to nudge her pen aside.

And let her see the heart upon my wing
And fold me out. The rest is suffering.

Guy Russell

POET FRIENDS
for Seamus, Andrew, Tony and Carol

I heard my good friend Jim was getting married
So I wrote a poem (as we poets do)
For Jimmy – he's a poet – and for Linda.
(And Linda is, of course, a poet too.)

It's nice in verse to make a little hi-there
To friends. And work that mentions them, it's true,
Goes down so well with editors who know them –
For all of them, of course, are poets too.

Where better could I advertise my contacts
With trad, hip, local, foreign, old and new?
For I like to mix with every kind of person
As long as they, of course, are poets too.

So if you judge my dedications cliquey
Or claim you feel excluded or non-U -
Take heart! We also might become friends soon, for
All you readers, of course, are poets too.

NIGHT OF THE UNREAD

The Heavens crash, the full moon hides its face,
The winds lash and the lightning's forks embrace

And in the literary graveyard – hark! – first, cries
From tombs whose names are long effaced, arise

Like souls in torment... Then the mosses writhe
As things which have been but are not alive

Exhume their yellow wasted bodies – look! –
In numbers like the leaves – of every book

Guy Russell

Ever put down. In vain these boundless hordes
Press forward, strain to thunder soundless words

As if to raving audiences, then pause
As if for gasps, or laughter, or applause.

Who are they? Surely they were never in
The immaculate Anthologies of Heaven?

They weren't. This is the Night of the Unread.
Unheard, unseen, their unloved forms are dead

But disinterred till dawn, to moan once more
In shadows of the light they floundered for.

Alas! Their sins were many: Feckless Cant.
Wilful Pretentiousness. Unstructured Rant.

Proud Obscurity. Commercial Pap.
Merciless Self-Indulgence. And Pure Crap.

Now they mould in musty bottom-drawers.
And more join them. More. And more. And more.

Will publishers sleep easily tonight?
A vision of the million souls who write

And millions more to come, born every day,
Filling bins and letterboxes on their way

To death, may haunt them faintly till they wake
With doleful groans and hellish bellyache,

But words of ghosts can't touch, or move. Their prints
Fade instantly... In damned indifference,

The heedless living sleep. The cold sun chases
The sad Unread back to their resting-places.

Guy Russell

CALLING

Yeah, was I such a jerk. The years I'd slack
To *Classic Metal Monsters* on the stack
Or scan *The Sun*, freeze honeys on Blind Date
Dig zits, play *Lemmings*, burp and flatulate
Till that cruel night when... Whoomph. Identify
What zapped my bedroom? Where it came from? Why?
I can't: my Gameboy crashed, the TV cracked,
The Sun caught fire, I paled as Cilla blacked
And bang in sync, those gold-disc dinosaurs
Roared and died out. And in that pause
Stood this bootgirl. White-faced with black curled locks,
Five foot in drains and twenty-six-hole Docs,
She rolled me backwards, strapped me to the bed,
Compressed my heart, put printblocks on my head
And as I screamed for death, in arty hate
She laughed and, with these words, revealed my fate:
"Oi, Guy! Employment Training time! I've booked
You proper work. You're mine." (At which she looked
Around my room, and smiled.) "Just as I heard:
Pathetic, shy" (slash) "dreamy" (slash slash) "nerd.
Yes, you're marked out for 'nature' and 'childhood'
'Fresh images', 'glimpses of life and mood';
Your frenzied mind will flush all hot about
Love, beauty, truth, and getting pamphlets out;
Your face will line like, oh like... virgin slate.
You'll be a scream, my lad, to educate."

A lightbulb seemed to ping above me. "NO–!
Please not–!" I cried. KER-PAF! Her plate-steel toe-
-Caps— OOF! "Please–" POW! KER-ZOW! "But I can't wri—"
Things blurred. The end. She'd stamped me in the eye
(Her print read "Passed") then waved this gold-nibbed wand
And signed me up. Limply, I intoned:

Later, a dusty photograph of Dad
Reminds me how we never talked. I'm sad.

She nodded musingly, and disappeared.
I woke with a strange urge to grow a beard.

Guy Russell

MUSHROOM PICKING

The end of September, and a fine bright day
after some rain is good. They spring that way
like magic in the fields. You look for them
to be like this small, with a white curly stem
and a little nipple on the top. An easy trip
out the city, there up beyond the airstrip
with the autumn colours, wow, so beautiful
and the cows munching mindlessly, eyes full
of this huge softness. Two hundred does us fine.
Ones with straight stems you should let alone.

Back home, we'll space them out on newspaper
checking each to see it's safe and proper
and removing odds of grass between the stalks.
We keep the cat away, because it likes
to nod out on *The Guardian*. Meg turns on
the gas fire and the kids' slot and is blown
through the round window. They taste shit though, fresh.
When they're dried I usually make a mush
to mix in party snacks with button-heads
the supermarket's brought up safe in sheds.

Mawuko Selormey

Mawuko Selormey

I AM NOT A DREAM

I am not a dream
I am realities destiny a spiritual flame
A ghost in the mist of ghouls that has no name
For you have stolen from me the only thing that exist
My soul it contains everything in me that consists
To you I am like a poison but did I mention my spirit
It connects through ribs, taken from another I can create
Let the earth combine to complete a full understanding of who I am
I too am a man and understand
Why separate my life from the chosen destiny that joins all of us
You let me be free on the streets but don't ever listen to me as an equal
In the office that you created I am but a whisper as the water cooler grasps for air
I rot away laid to waste, just an emergency flair for coffee an entity that needs to be filled with more files
Let the sun see my soul and attach itself to my remains as my final goal
For as I live here all you see now is my dream
The dream of me being equal and living in unity with them
And as they cast me to dust some let their sorrow weep
But they burn me to dust.
They burn what remains and now I am nothing but tamed
Tamed from my inner ear that was calling my to be their dream
But the future is foreseen all I am is a dream just a dream
I have become what I did not want to be a slow tranquil thought dying away
Hey to everyone who knew me let's just say he was a dream and he reminded me of us and who we could be.
A source of supreme light, wisdom and unity
We will remember him yes we will remember him.

Mawuko Selormey

Gloomy souls enter a colourful world
And low and behold are transformed
With thoughts like gold
Light races, smiles on happy faces
Dance steps blossom as elegance graces the street
No longer do grandmothers weep
The culture man creeps
And enlightens a path for children to follow
Concerned minds are set at ease
Worried minds become hollow and the system sparks into life
What was set undercover blossoms?
And goodness is rife
A good deed here and there
A culture that is laid down in squares
Become hypnotic, roundabouts alight
Places names are full of new houses which take in the chosen few
Who are trapped by the magical entity of the cities voodoo?
Do you walk through this magical land?
That knows itself as Milton Keynes beautifully transformed from wasteland.
Well if you are give yourselves a smile
For now there are 200,000 people with every time with your unique style.

Mawuko Selormey

PRECIOUS STONES

Precious stones lie in water
Eroding in times order
Earth fluctuates and pulsates
Expected to be remembered for its trouble but all we do is lay waste and create rubble
From a perfectly serene feel
What is the deal?
What is the deal?
With the 9 to 5's
Unseen highs and mountains to climb
Royal families and royal tribes why can't we just express our lives rather than hide
Take a stand and unwind
Maybe we will do justice to time
And save a world that has been hurt by human crimes
Just once if we stop and see what is going on?
We might repair the heartache
That for a generation has been so wrong

ACTIONS, MEMORIES AND WORDS

You can communicate to many people, in many tongues
But what transpires through your heart and out of your lungs
Can only sustain a sound
To make sure your soul touches everyone around
You must sense the one rhythm the one beat
To say Bonjour, Guten Tag, Buenos Dias will only make people move their feet
For a moment
For the wind will just blow away the sounds along with the leaves that chant your name
To speak, to remember, and to know what someone means is a language free of fame.
You must learn their rhythm and their dance
Their words to you must fixate your vision with enlightenment at first glance
For to communicate means more than words
It transpires every emotion from within your soul that can be stirred.

Mawuko Selormey

MIDSUMMER TREE

My leaves sway
Ever since the month of May
As you walk and talk through Midsummer place
A gentle wind blows at its own pace
Making me swing to the groove
Letting flowers blossom with petals colourful and bees on the move
Sit down next to me
And have a lovely cup of English tea
The summer days set my mood and as couples tweak their relationship making up after feuds
The rain sets me free and allows me to breathe
And as I shake my branches cows settle down around eating my loose leaves
Life picks up about five and workers are entertained by my beauty
They see something else of me strength, peace and tranquillity
The day marches on and as the sun sets I breathe to sleep
For security will make sure I have good memories to keep, good memories to keep.

SOUNDS OF LOVE

The version of sound enters the soul
It could be a sweet whisper that enlightens the ear hole
Lifts a smile to the cheeks
And makes the laugh extra sweet
The rise of the chest
Is such a laugh at best
Taken in by the sound of tapping feet
Just hear the sound of love as it speaks.

Richard Skellington

Richard Skellington was born in St Anne's, Nottingham, in 1948. For the past 34 years he has worked for the Open University. He edits Society Matters (see http://www.open.ac.uk/socialsciences/about-the-faculty/society-matters/society-matters.php?), writes a regular blog for the BBC (see http://www.open2.net/blogs/society/index.php?blog=10&author=63), and is a university administrator. Richard authored the best selling book Race in Britain Today (published by Sage, 1996). He has been a councillor on Stony Stratford Town Council for the last 8 years, and lived in the town since 1981. Richard is keen cricket lover and umpires in the Thames Valley League, and for the Buckinghamshire Cricket Association. Richard has acted in many local drama productions between 1976 and 2005, and has produced and directed several plays in Milton Keynes, including Hedda Gabler, The Importance of Being Earnest, The Elephant Man, and The Tragedy of King Richard the Third. He began to write poetry seriously in 2007.

Richard Skellington

EXIT STRATEGY

His blood had long since dried on rock and sand
In this wretched war, in another's land
His exit strategy was clear it seemed
We should not question, nor condemn his dreams
His relatives have been informed, so please, no fuss
Over this other tommy, gone to dust
Shed no crocodile tears for him
He laughed and loved like us; he's smiled his last
He's gone to his other world.
He knew his government murdered children in its sleep
For sake of safer steers back home
And hearts and minds that know their own
He's at peace now back in Wootton Bassett
He's left the land of bombs and shattered dreams
Its nightmares darken, his are at an end
What did his letter say?
War is organised murder
And as his union-flagged coffin, cap decked, passes mourners' eyes
No minister stares down with false goodbyes

THE SUNDAY VISIT

One dies of war, I like any old disease
A Terre Wilfred Owen
For my father
In school playgrounds down the hill
Children's voices could still be heard
Let's see where the mad will be
I know, I know
Up the hill in Mapperley

Richard Skellington

I

On wet Sunday afternoons
Long after the War that killed him
A gaunt figure dressed in soiled
Ill-fitting clothes urine stained
Stands silent and alone
Outside the lobotomy ward
Bent double shuffling in carpet slippers
He moves slowly down the long dark corridor
Towards the distant square of light
Rocking gently forward and back
Lips hanging onto the cigarette
Recently rolled with trembling hands
Between Rizla paper number three
He stops outside the asylum shop
Locked
It was a Sunday after all
And staring at the rows of forbidden Woodbines
Lined on yonder wall
His trembling fingers remove a match
From a tattered England Glory box
Twice he strikes the match
On the third strike it lights
The flame arches upwards towards the cigarette tip
His lungs devour all, no smoke exhales
And like all the rest he scavenged
The ashtrays of the wards
For tiny fag ends extinguished by lost souls
Between nicotine burnt fingers
His butt glows red in the dark, soon
The dregs of the condemned were gone
And Stanley's slippers did the rest
His haunted brow frowned
Troubled now by murmurs from beyond the war
He stumbles towards the light
Thinking of the Ghurkha who gave him tea

Richard Skellington

II

He reached a junction where
The endless corridors crossed
Eyes turned toward the purple wall
Painted dark like all the rest

III

Look you can see the solitary inmates there
Walking in circles speaking to themselves
Frantically rubbing their hands twitching
Some stare catatonically into the abyss
Others like statues stand
Listen. You can hear their whispers
Suddenly a terrifying scream
Pierces the babble but no one jumps
Is it the fairground's laughing policeman
Smell the acrid air of human waste
In soiled clothes, smell, please do
Windows all are locked tight
Stale tobacco clings to carpet and chair
The morning's disinfectant does not reach
The lingering faint stench of excrement

IV

You can't help but stare, you can't
A frail woman older than her years
Cleans imaginary windows
Hands gently removing the last spot
Of invisible dust from the imagined pane
Stanley sees see his children in the light
Holding their mother's hand
He stoops and tenderly kisses their cheeks
His daughter flinches as his stumbled chin
Meets her soft pink skin
Mother's lips meet his
The boy freezes, still

Richard Skellington

V
A conversation.
Did Notts County win
No they lost four-nil
And then nothing, just silence for
Two hours until the final bell
No other visitors came
Time ticks so slowly
Stanley's Sunday confession splits the air
'Did I tell you about the Ghurkha?
In the jungle he brought me tea
From a corned beef tin,
He saved my life'
Stanley stopped abruptly
On hearing more genocidal echoes from the war
He stared back into the abyss

VI
The leaving bell tolled thrice
And rising mother boy and girl waved goodbye
The boy turned around to see his father's nicotine fingers
Close the curtain
On the phantom window cleaner
Wheeling in the shadows
And Stanley was gone.

In school playgrounds down the hill
Children's voices could still be heard
Let's see where the mad will be
I know, I know
Up the hill in Mapperley

*Mapperley is a suburb on a high hill to north of the city of Nottingham.
It was one of the largest asylums in Britain before it closed in the1980s.*

Richard Skellington

THE LAST SUPPER

Before the last dust had settled
On the war just before last
The leaders came over to dinner
While the world gazed on aghast
In Gaza buried under rubble
The old and young did they lay
They had nothing to eat but each other
No crumbs from a world far away
As leaders ate at their banquet
And the ink on the ceasefire dried
Clawed hands picked on the vanquished
And tore the last flesh from their eyes
And when the table was emptied
And only the bones there were left
They all drank Napoleon brandy
And toasted the war after next

matthew michael taylor

matthew michael taylor, 34½, is the editor of cult magazine *Monkey Kettle* – delivering poetry, prose and, er... other stuff to the outskirts of the UK poetry world since 1999 – and is one of the core members of the Monkey Kettle collective who regularly pepper the grid-roads of MK with arts events, gigs, plays, exhibitions and anything else that takes their fancy. He is also the singer in "MK's Premier Acoustic Duo": *The Further Adventures Of Vodka Boy*.

MMT is almost ridiculously proud of being one of the first generation of writers & artists to grow up in Milton Keynes. He's currently Secretary of the Board of Trustees at MADCAP Performing Arts Centre in Wolverton and a member of the Arts Gateway MK Literature Panel. But despite this apparent 'elder statesman' status of the local arts scene, he's definitely still cool too. For real. Innit. No diggety.

www.monkeykettle.co.uk   mmtmk.blogspot.com

matthew michael taylor

TOMMY HEMLOCK

Sainsbury's latest tagline is
"Try something new today"
So I decided to throw myself
Full-bodied, full-force
Into their household furnishings
Display of tabletop mirrors.
I made sure I broke as many
As possible by flailing out
With my feet and hands as
I hit the shelves.
Stone me.
What a life.
The shards went everywhere,
Broken glass and silver metal
Scattering across the Bathroom aisle.
I guess there were cuts and lacerations
But I was too busy to register
the pain, too busy gleefully
counting up in sevens inside my head.
As the tannoy burst into life
Somewhere in the distance,
I slid and crumpled to the floor
Where I gently but deliberately
Lay myself safely on my left side
Knee forward, head downward
Putting myself into the
Recovery position.

PORTENTS

There's two magpies and a dove
Outside our flat in a tree
And I don't understand how no-one else sees the significance of this
But me

matthew michael taylor

HEY KID

hey kid
does something hurt?
your heart?
was it something bad
you think you did?
try not to be so sad
hey kid
hey kid
forever seeing red
and feeling torn apart
all hope inert
and yes the misery has spread
and yes the death of joy and love and art
hey kid
hey kid
i guess i'm old enough to be your dad
(despite this shirt)
and i've already played your part
i've got a reasonable clue what's coming up ahead
so maybe even wisdom to impart
hey kid
hey kid
when we are twice as smart
life won't be half as bad
our nights less filled with creeping dread
the horror hid
cos you and me we're both just hominid
hey kid
hey kid
so there's torment always boiling in your head?
get rid
get up out of your bed
shed the dirt
embrace your life instead
hey kid
hey
kid
i reckon you'll be glad
you did

matthew michael taylor

REGRETSONG

i drift around
an empty flat
looking for some sign of you
found one of your eyelashes
in a kitchen drawer
i don't know how they get there but they do

it took me nine bad months
just to figure out where we went wrong
and by the time i did it was nine bad months
since you'd been gone

i drift around
an empty town
knock on each and every door
none of the people will say
where you are now
just that you're happy, not like before

it took me eight bad years
just to figure out where we went wrong
and by the time i did it was eight bad years
since you'd been gone

i drift around
an empty world
and everywhere i scream your name
i'll do everything that you wanted of me
if you'll just come back alive again

it took me all my life
just to figure out where we went wrong
and by the time i did it was all my life
since you'd been gone

Alex Toms

Alex Toms, 33, now lives near Colchester in Essex because she prefers Roman ruins to Concrete Cows. She remembers Milton Keynes as the place where a lot of things went wrong for her, but on a more positive note, the place where, thanks to *Monkey Kettle* and *Tongue in Chic*, she fell in love with poetry. She has had poems published in *Monkey Kettle* and *Writers' Forum*, and having lost her open mic virginity at the inaugural T*ongue in Chic*, enjoys performing her poetry in public, these days at the *Poetry Wivenhoe* sessions.

Alex has a nine-year-old son who is nearly as tall as she is.

Alex Toms

GRID SYSTEM

Cars — silver beads
shoot in all directions,
like mercury
from a broken thermometer,
or bullets from an AK-47
intent on nothing but their target.
All day and night this city moves,
while I hover
like a needle on a compass,
striving to find True North.
Milton Keynes is a well-oiled machine,
the roundabouts its cogs.
Cars drop off obediently
at the right exits,
and go on their way. The Grid System
means nothing to me. H9, V10
unfinished equations.
The roads stretch on forever,
with little to distinguish
one from another.
There is never silence,
only the incessant
rushing of the cars.
If I could,
I would make my own Grid System,
and like the travellers of old,
plot the position of the stars.

Alex Toms

THE FEMALE ICARUS

If Daedalus made for me a pair
of shining, peacock feather wings,
I wouldn't try to reach the sun, but wait
instead to feel a coolness in the air,
then venture out with keen-eyed, fluttering things.
The night will hide my learner's shame, as time
and time again, I tumble to the ground.
But soon my body, bruised and aching, will
be lifted from the earth, and slowly rise
into the sky. My wings will match
the beating of my heart, as I ascend
to where the stars regard me with
unblinking eyes. I feel their pity as I'm drawn
to face the judgement of the moon.

RAPUNZEL GOES TO THE HAIRDRESSER'S

After he left her
for a girl with a boyish crop,
Rapunzel decided
it was time for a change.
The receptionist wearing the Flawless Finish Foundation
and the acrylic nails,
raised one perfectly plucked eyebrow and said,
It's going to take a lot of work.
Sitting before a mirror
that magnified every zit, Rapunzel watched
the reflections of the stylists
as they buzzed around her in tight black T-shirts shrieking,
Look at those split ends!
Then it happened.
The one they called Shanice
ran her fingers through Rapunzel's hair,
and an ivy leaf came loose,
and floated to the ground.

Alex Toms

This was not so strange (after all,
it was a windy autumn day). But then
she combed out a bootlace
belonging to the Prince, then
one of the Witch's green pointed fingernails.
The Saturday girl stopped sweeping the floor.
Shanice got out her scissors then, and cut
a golden rope of hair right off.
A mouse fell down with it,
and scuttled off across the floor.
She sliced and chopped
for three whole hours,
during which time she found
a nest of fledgling birds,
mouldy half eaten chocolates,
three hairbrushes,
used condoms
and a book of romantic verse.

When Rapunzel finally left,
light headed in her halo of hairspray,
Shanice realised she hadn't paid.
She was still sweeping up her hair at midnight.

TODAY I SHALL

Not break down.
Instead, I will take a bus to town.
When I get there,
I will toss back my hair,
lift my chin
and feel my earrings swing.
But as I walk among the lost and the forlorn,
I know I'll be inevitably drawn
to the local library,
and the shadowy shelves of poetry.

Darren Turney

Thrown out of english at school for having a "personality".
so no apologies if my poems aint perfect gramatically!
Hope you enjoy them, but i dont really care...
never wrote them for you to share!

Darren Turney

LOONEY TUNES

Fuck this illness,
Surrounded by stillness,
Busy doing nothing worn out by everything
Trying so hard going backwards by yards.
Fuck this illness,
I don't want to lose
It grew over time, something I did not chose
It creeps up at night whilst stirring my sight.
Fuck this illness
It brings everyone down
They try so hard just running around
Everyone loves me all so much, but is this really quite enough
Fuck this illness
I really will win
But oh so hard when covered in sin
Bollocks to this I will force another biscuit in
Fuck this illness
I don't like me.
Remove all the mirrors then I can't see
Lose five stone!? ... tee hee hee.
Fuck this illness
Easier to give in
But who will then really win?
There is a simple choice in life, sink or swim!!!

Darren Turney

D.I.V.O.R.C.E... becomes final today...

Have you ever been through a divorce???
Mental fucking torture at full G-force
Targeting one another without any remorse
But it wasn't her... it was all me of course!!!
So where did it go wrong?
Was it ever good? Did we leave it too long?!
What about those hazy days listening to our favourite songs,
I think I was made to care and love, not to be tough or strong!?
But how do you show that, when life moves at 100 miles per hour
It always turns to screaming and in the corner my dog cowers.
Cant please everyone, WHY did it turn sour?
Have we always hated each other and just hidden it with flowers?
Gets to the point where I want to just pack and piss-off, peace I yearn,
Walk away from everything and never ever return
But that happened to me and not good for my kids to learn
So I stick out another argument about what I pay and what I earn.
When I was 14 my parents separated,
Asking me who I wanted to live with, they should never have mated!
Then I wouldn't have been in that position and couldn't have hated
Now history is repeating itself, at 18 I should have been castrated!!!
Remove all emotion and leave me be
Bored as fuck but from the pain I will be free
Referred to me, myself and I, not WE
Claim my 2 daughters and make a team of three.
So I will ask again...Have you ever been through a divorce???
Mental fucking torture at full G-force
Targeting one another without any remorse
But it wasn't me... it was all her of course!!!

Darren Turney

COS IT WAS LOVE,- LOVE, -LOVE AT FIRST SIGHT...

She fell in love at the biscott mill
Whilst snuggling me, sitting under the window sill
The whole pub empty, the place so still
Fun and vivacious, with drop dead gorgeous looks that could kill
We stole our first kiss whilst sitting on a bench
So young and naïve, the kiss was long and French.
From above I believed an angel had been sent
To make me embrace life and never ever resent.
I was a chef and she was a barmaid
Who ever said they were an easy lay?
We would chat and cuddle and in the same bed we would stay
But not so that we could have a quick "roll in the hay".
I wanted to hold her tight for the rest of my life
I knew straight away that this one would be my wife
Working in a pub, the rumours are rife
Is the fit girl behind the bar really going out with the poof with the knife?
The poof with the knife, made cracking Pizza's.
Made funky ice-cream with bits of maltesers
When she came in the kitchen, we would snuggle in the freezer
I think she knew then that I would never leave her.
It baffled most people, me included!
But to nearly all, my qualities had eluded
But not from Sarah who saw my feet were rooted
To the first rung of the ladder to become suited and booted
I loved her so much, it was never a chore
Although love is blind, I could see all her flaws
I accepted them all and never asked for more
Because she really was straight out of the "top drawer"
18 years and the love is still so strong.
The problem is something went wrong
Life took over and now she is gone
Mental illness is cruel; she has suffered for far too long.
So does this mean I am no longer smitten?
Will we not grow old together and keep smelly kittens?
retire to Spain away from chilly Britain,
You will have to read the last verse... which is yet to be written!!!...

Darren Turney

GREED!

Why is everybody so fucking greedy?
Want, want, want, ... so bloody needy!
One dimension is no good, it has to be 3-D
You have to conform to the "norm" or else you appear cheesy.
Do all these possessions make you happy?
Wives work hard and are much more snappy
No time for their kids, they pay people to change the nappy
Don't want to listen to stories on the knees of their pappy.
They would rather sit all day and play X-box.
Moan like fuck, if for Christmas they get socks
Expect at least one expensive frock
Then with no respect they run amok!
What are we teaching them, what are we creating?
I see so many kids and I wish their fathers had done more masturbating!
How do we stop the greed gene, it is so frustrating...
When the money runs out, I will be waiting!
I have a house and my wife has a house
Some people can't afford to put food in their mouth
Told to get on their bike and for work, head south
Trying to turn a coin as they jostle and joust.
In the old days they stole just to put "steam" on the table
The economy then was very unstable
But they helped one another and were always able
To love, help and look out for each other, NOT brag about a designer label.
But once you succeed
You have time to look up and breathe
Perhaps I could spend time with kids to plant a seed
And try and get through to them what they really need
But I feel like, in the wind I am pissing
Until they get here they wont realise what they are missing
They know everything already so why would they be listening
To a silly old twat writing poetry and of a nicer world simply wishing.

Brian Two

Brian began performing in stand up comedy in 1997. Within a year or so he was performing across the country and became resident MC at The Clock Inn for Comedy in Milton Keynes. He also began working for Paramount in 1998 and travelled the length and breadth of the country as MC and performer in various comedy venues from the Comedy Store in Leicester Square to the Edinburgh Fringe.

More recently Brian has appeared in the world stage premier of the TV series *Ripping Yarns*, created by Michael Palin and Terry Jones. In addition he is a regular member of the improvisation group *Whose Turn Is It Anyway?* Brian has always written poems and songs as part of his set. These are meant to be read as performance pieces.

Brian Two

When my son was no more that four years old, he would prefix all his statements to me with "my daddy" rather than the traditional "daddy" or "dad". The following poem was written to capture that time of innocence.

O MY DADDY

O my daddy, you know all the secrets
About life and what makes the world spin
About the sun the rain and the flowers
The calm the storm and the winds

You know why dogs need injections
And the car won't start in the cold
But O my daddy, will you still have the answers
When you're hairless and fat and are old

O my daddy, there'll be times when I'll need you
When I'm poorly or tired and cold
We will sit and drink soup by the fire
And look to each other to hold

I wish son, I had all the answers
About the meaning of time and of life
But to me son it's all an enigma
You'd best ask your mother, my wife.

My son is now seventeen and I am working on a second poem called "Dad, you know f**k all..."

Brian Two

The best way to read this poem is whilst sitting in a wing chair, wearing a Pam Ayres wig and attempting a Norfolk accent. This is the persona I adopted when I wrote it as a homage to the great poet herself.

BOGIES

I blow my nose into a tissue
Then look to see what I've produced.
Sometimes my bogies are sticky
And some times my bogies are loose.

When blowing your nose, use a tissue.
You'll always find that it is best.
If you blow your nose with no tissue,
You may get it over your chest

There are yellow and green and some red ones
Depending on how well you are.
The worst place to pick out a bogie
Is sat at the lights in your car.
You open the window to flick it
The lights they turn green on the street
You can't find a home for that bogie
So you just pop it under the seat

Now rich folks don't produce bogies
For rich folks don't produce snot
They have someone who comes round
And cleans out their nose
But I am just poor...and have not.

Brian Two

This is a poem I wrote with my son on a sunny afternoon on a bench in my garden in 2003. I perform this poem in the voice of Peter Sellers playing an old man

MODERN MANNERS

I sat in the garden. I broke wind and said pardon
For that is what gentlemen do.
I'd had too many beans,
They'd upset my spleen,
And I'd covered the bench with poo

My wife said, that's it,
It's all covered in s**t
You can clean up your self if you please.
She was probably right, it was a horrible sight
And it had run down the back of my knees

So I called for the cleaner
Who had cooked me that dinner
It was her fault, the silly old cow.
There's a horrible stink
As she stands at the sink...
She's washing my trousers now.

Lionel Welch

Aged 65 and happily retired; I have lived in Milton Keynes since 1977.

I suppose that it is because I have been a political and trade union activist all my working life that my work is mainly of a revolutionary style. I rarely do nice or funny.

I believe I have seen the best and the worst of times in Britain, and that is what has influenced my poetry.

I began writing and performing in October 2008, and have since, when time permits, played an active part in the local poetry scene.

All credit is due to *Tongue in Chic*, and *Poetry Kapow* for giving me the necessary help and support, and a platform to perform on.

Lionel Welch

ARISE

Hear the beat of the workers, rhythmically drumming,
Can't you feel the revolution coming?
Our bright coloured banners raised on high
Unfurled and swirling against the sky
We've had enough of your capitalist state
With your wars of race and religion, engineered hate
They're not about the peoples' need
But to satisfy your bottomless greed
Everyone's the same, regardless of creed or colour of skin
To claim otherwise is the original sin
So brother and sister, sister and brother
Stand up together, link arms with each other
Let's show the bastards that they'll never beat us
While we stand firm together, they'll never defeat us

Lionel Welch

A LETTER TO SIR FRED GOODWIN

Dear Sir Fred, I'm a pensioner too,
But thanks to you and all your mates, I'll never be well off like you
Forty none years of my life spent working,
Doing my duty, never shirking

Then you gambled with our pensions, our savings and our ISAs,
In plain old fashioned language,
You're a shower of bloody twicers

You did it all to get rich quick,
And here's the part that makes us sick,
As we struggle food, fuel and council tax to afford,
You'll be relaxing in some luxury resort abroad

If I had my way I'd strip you of your assets, house, car and pension,
And then I'd go to work, with tools, on bits too rude to mention

The truth is your greed for profit maximisation
Has brought devastation to the nation,
Now how about some compensation
Allow us to live in dignity, without financial deprivation

You and all your banker chums have got us in this mess
And you couldn't care less
That we've got no redress

So I'll sign off finally,
Yours sincerely
In poverty

Lionel Welch

THE VETERAN

I was barely a man when they called me,
They promised action, adventure and fun.
So I joined, we trained hard for six weeks,
And the bastards gave me a gun.
"Come lads," they said,
"There's a job to be done in a far away land."
And we flew round the world
To a place called Helmand
We fought bravely at first,
But our kit was the worst,
Nothing worked, food was short, life was cheap,
Limbs were blown off, comrades were killed, the bodies piled up in a heap.
I was shot in the spine,
But they said "You'll be fine, we'll fly you home and give you good care."
But when I got home, the story had changed, the money was needed elsewhere.
"You're lucky," they said,
Though I' rather be dead,
"At least you escaped with your life"
But here in this wheelchair, unable to move,
I'm no fucking use to my wife.
In a small terraced house, on a run down estate,
With benefits set at the lowest rate, while they wallow in the greed
Of their capitalist greed,
Is it surprising my only emotion is hate?
So don't fall for their story
Of adventure and glory,
It's just another political lie,
They'll stay home and get rich,
While you bleed in a ditch,
And toast you in champagne if you die.

Lionel Welch

DEVIL WOMAN

Thirty years ago, a woman called Thatcher,
AKA the school milk snatcher,
Came to power in this realm,
With evil intent she took the helm
She said that all the British workers
Were a bunch of lazy shirkers
She turned our lives into a financial gamble
Where the bulls and bears of the Stock exchange were free to ramble
She privatised our railway lines,
Closed down our factories and our mines,
Maggie, Hitler in World War Two
Never did as much damage as you
To our economy
She split communities apart,
She really showed she had no heart,
With millions of workers on the dole,
While she sold off our oil, gas, and coal
She banned Trade Unions at factory gates
From showing loyalty to their mates
When in dispute with the boss,
She really didn't give a toss
For solidarity or society
Nothing was sacred or out of her range,
She gave all to the wide boys in the Stock Exchange,
Schools and hospitals were privatised,
But services were worse, not revitalised
She said "The lady's not for turning",
If I had my way she'd have been for burning,

Lionel Welch

As she stole from the poor to give to the rich,
She really was the Devil's bitch
Interest rates stood at fifteen percent,
While millions out of work couldn't pay their rent,
If you needed a job, she said "Take a hike,
Leave your family and get on your bike."
Now she's old, bent, withered and all alone,
Just like some medieval crone,
May a curse be on her bones,
Maggie Thatcher.

When she dies, we'll organise a rave,
And all dance barefoot on her grave,
As for her schemes and deeds infernal,
Her soul's consumed in fires eternal

Lightning Source UK Ltd.
Milton Keynes UK
27 May 2010

154816UK00002B/1/P